TAX SHELTERS

TAX SHELTERS
Choose with care!

W. E. McLeod, M.B.A.

International Self-Counsel Press Ltd.
Head and Editorial Office
Vancouver
Toronto   Seattle

Printed in Canada.
First edition: January, 1977
Tenth edition: November, 1985
Eleventh edition: January, 1987

Canadian Cataloguing in Publication Data

McLeod, W. E. (William E.), 1941-
    Tax shelters: choose with care!

(Self-counsel series)
First-2nd eds. published as: Tax savings plans in Canada; 3rd-7th eds. published as: Tax shelters in Canada; 8th ed. published as: Tax shelters for Canadians.
ISBN 0-88908-651-6

    1. Tax shelters - Canada - Popular works. 2. Tax planning - Canada - Popular works. 3. Registered Retirement Savings Plans.*
I. Title. II. Series.
KE5683.Z82M234 1986   332.6'042   C86-091590-5

Cover props courtesy of Canada Umbrella Ltd., 120 West 3rd Avenue, Vancouver, B.C. V5Y 1E9

International Self-Counsel Press Ltd.
Head and Editorial Office
306 West 25th Street
North Vancouver, British Columbia   V7N 2G1
Vancouver   Toronto   Seattle

CONTENTS

LIST OF TABLES

INTRODUCTION

The eleventh edition of *Tax Shelters* is characterized by extensive changes and proposed changes to the Income Tax Act. The February 26, 1986 federal budget proposed sweeping changes to the way Registered Retirement Savings Plans (RRSPs) are terminated. In June, 1986, Revenue Canada announced more changes to the proposals that were tabled in the May, 1985 budget. With tax legislation this undecided, consumers would be well advised to check with Revenue Canada on any questions with which they are uncomfortable.

A summary of the many recent tax changes will provide some insight into how the world of personal financial management has changed and where it seems to be going.

First, very few Canadians realize what inflation has done to many tax deductions. For example, the $1 000 tax-free investment income and the $1 000 tax-free pension income have never been indexed since they were introduced in 1972. In mid-1986, these deductions were worth only $333 of their original $1 000 value. The $3 500 and $5 500 RRSP deductions were last indexed in 1976 and in mid-1985 were worth only approximately $1 646 and $2 587 respectively. In 1984, the $100 of undocumented charitable deductions, which was never indexed, was abolished.

The federal budget of May 23, 1985 continued, and perhaps accelerated, the trend to fewer tax breaks in Canada. With the stroke of a pen, Canada's best tax shelter, the Registered Home Ownership Savings Plan (RHOSP) went down the drain. Tax-sheltered RHOSP funds were returned to taxpayers to spend as they wish.

Income-splitting was eliminated as well. Transferring investment income to a lower-income spouse was one of Canada's more popular tax dodges. It was used mostly by upper-income taxpayers, but many average Canadians with over $1 000 in annual investment income were beginning to realize the benefits of income-splitting. A dependent spouse could have earned $520 in 1986 before the deduction declared by the supporting spouse began to diminish. This, in effect, meant that the $1 000 of tax-free investment income would have increased to $1 520.

The May 23, 1985 budget proposed that, beginning in the taxation year 1986, pension income would no longer qualify as earned income. This meant that individuals living on pension income, RRSP income, and investment income would be unable to contribute to a spousal RRSP. Beginning in 1990, pension income was not to be eligible for transfer to an RRSP. People who take up second or retirement careers would no longer be able to defer tax on their pension income. Nor would they be able to annuitize RRSP funds and roll the annuity income back into their RRSP. This meant that decisions to turn RRSP funds into a life income would become final and irrevocable, regardless of what happened to interest rates. This proposed change was postponed in June of 1986 and the old rules will apply, at least for 1986.

Not all of the May 23, 1985 budget was bad news for personal financial planning. For example, individuals can now turn RRSP funds into a life income regardless of age. Prior to the budget, this could not be done before age 60. Curiously, the minister did not apply the same logic to the maximum age that RRSPs could be purchased or held. That maximum remains at December 31 of the year in which the planholder turns 71.

For individuals who do not belong to a registered pension plan, the budget proposed to substantially increase RRSP contributions beginning in 1986. The increases will take full effect in 1990.

These two changes will mean that the scramble for RRSP investment dollars will become more intense, more unscrupulous, more expensive, more misleading, and more confusing. Good luck consumer!

Beginning in 1986, unused RRSP contributions can be carried forward for a period of up to seven years. This may or may not be a good idea. But it certainly appeals to certain mutual fund salespeople and stockbrokers. They are busily engaged in a campaign to encourage the public to take advantage of this apparent concession. This issue is examined in depth in the section on mutual funds.

There has also been a change to the capital gains tax structure by allowing Canadians to accumulate up to $500 000 in capital gains over a lifetime without attracting tax of any kind, and a number of significant shifts in investment and tax planning should occur.

Funds earmarked for RRSPs or debt reduction may well be re-directed toward a pool of common stocks, a mutual fund, a second home, a farm or some other type of real estate investment.

Perhaps one of the most significant changes in the field of personal financial management was proposed in the February 26, 1986 budget. The rules governing Registered Retirement Income Funds (RRIFs) were changed to allow minimum contributions and to remove the limit of one RRIF per person.

Prior to the May budget, mutual funds and common stock lost their preferential tax treatment when they were placed behind the RRSP tax shelter. The new budget makes it less attractive to use equity types of investments for RRSP purposes. This will hurt those individuals who have followed this strategy and those who are thinking about it. It will also hurt mutual funds and many people who sell them. People who make their living buying and selling common stocks will have more difficulty in persuading their customers to put the stock into a self-administered RRSP.

The net effect of recent changes to the Income Tax Act is not easy to assess. But it seems fair to point out that two things appear to have happened. First, the net tax burden has increased. And second, that burden is being shifted away from high-income earners toward lower- and middle-income earners. The abolition of the capital gains tax for almost everyone and the dramatic forthcoming increases in tax deductible RRSP contributions will accelerate this trend.

Accompanying the shift in the tax burden is an increasing reliance on regressive taxes for government revenues. Hidden sales taxes, excise taxes on fuel, alcohol and tobacco all hit lower-income people harder than higher-income people. We have become accustomed to these taxes and we accept the increases seemingly without note, comment or complaint. Recent governments, with these profound tax changes, have cleverly extracted more and more revenue from three classes of citizens — those who don't know what is happening, those who don't care and those who know but who are helpless and cannot fight back. Tax planning and financial management are now, more than ever before, crucial priorities for every Canadian.

1
REGISTERED RETIREMENT SAVINGS PLANS

a. HOW DO RRSPs WORK?

Registered retirement savings plans (RRSPs) came into existence in 1957 as a result of legislation passed by the government of John Diefenbaker. Prior to 1957, the only Canadians who could make contributions to a pension plan and deduct the contributions from taxable income were those who were fortunate enough to have employers who provided such plans to their employees.

However, the game changed in 1957 with the coming of registered retirement savings plans. Under the new legislation, Canadians could make contributions to a broad range of investment programs, declare those investments as their personal pension plans and, subject to certain dollar limitations, deduct the contributions from their taxable incomes. In addition to setting up a scheme for people to establish their own pension plans, the legislation allowed citizens who were already eligible for pensions through their employers to set up supplementary plans.

Those who are not members of a company pension plan can contribute annually the lesser of $5 500 or 20% of earned income and deduct these contributions from their taxable incomes. For supplementary plans, the legislation allows deductible contributions of the lesser of $3 500 or 20% of earned income minus contributions by individuals to their pension plans. The lower limit of $3 500 also applies to those who are members of employer pension plans where the employee makes no contribution. In June, 1986, Revenue Canada announced that proposed changes in contribution limits were being postponed and that the old limits would apply in 1986 for members of Registered Pension Plans. For non-members, the 1986 limit will be raised to $7 500.

b. OTHER IMPORTANT PROPOSED CHANGES TO RRSPs

1. Definition of earned income

The new definition of earned income, which is the type of income that is important for determining RRSP contributions, has the following components:

(a) Income from all sources of employment before the deduction of contributions to unemployment insurance, Canada and Quebec pension plans, and registered pension plans, but net of all expenses or losses

(b) Income from all business carried on either alone or as a partner actively engaged in the business, net of any losses during the year

(c) Royalties for a work or invention of which the tax filer was the author or inventor

(d) Net research grants

(e) Registered supplementary unemployment insurance benefits

(f) Amounts received as alimony or maintenance; amounts paid as alimony or maintenance will be deducted in determining earned income

This change in definition will hurt individuals who have retired and, for whatever reason, never contributed to a spousal RRSP. Under the old rules, pension income qualified as earned income. Therefore, up to 20% of earned income or $5 500, whichever was less, could be put into a spousal RRSP up to the year in which the individual turned 71. Pension income could be transferred to a spouse to allow the spouse to annuitize the plan and take advantage of the $1 000 of tax-free pension income each year after the spouse turned 65. This strategy is another casualty of the May 23 budget.

However, these proposed changes were postponed in June of 1986 and the old definition of earned income will apply, at least for 1986.

2. Transfers of pension income to RRSPs

Under current law, transfer of pension income to RRSPs can be made without limits. Several types of pension

6

income are eligible for this type of transfer. Payments from an annuitized RRSP, payments from a registered pension plan, and payments from the Canada and Quebec pension plans and old age security all qualify. The budget proposes that tax-free pension transfers be permitted only up to the amount of an individual's unused room. To allow transitional relief, this change will not come into effect until January 1, 1990.

This change will eventually eliminate three important tax planning strategies. First, many individuals retire early with lucrative pensions from fire departments, police forces, the armed forces, and from the public service. They often take up second careers and transfer all or most of their pension income to RRSPs to be used as pension income when their second careers are over and when they are in their lowest tax bracket. This practice will be eliminated by 1990.

Second, many people retire shortly before age 65 and do not take up a second career. There may, in some of these cases, be a time period of two or three years before they reach age 65, and therefore have a full calendar year in which they receive only their pension income and also the extra deduction for being age 65. A good strategy for these individuals under the old rules was to live on some of their savings and dump their pension income into an RRSP. Then they could take funds out at the low tax rate after age 65 or leave them to further accumulate and add to the amount that could eventually be turned into a form of life income also to be taxed at the lowest rate possible. After 1990 this strategy will not be possible.

Finally, many people annuitize their RRSPs well before age 71 and plow the annuity income right back into another RRSP. They do this for two reasons. First, they want to protect themselves against an anticipated drop in interest rates which, as we all know, sometimes happens and sometimes does not. Second, they may do it on the advice of an annuity salesperson who may persuade them to do this not once but a number of times. It may or may not prove to be a good tactic for the individual but it is very lucrative for the salesperson who picks up a commission of

7

3% of the amount of money involved each time the annuity is purchased.

The budget not only wipes out this strategy as of 1990, it forces individuals to guess what will happen to future interest rates. When the new rules come into effect, RRSPs can only be annuitized once. This is perhaps one of the harshest and least discussed aspects of the budget.

3. Transfer of retirement allowances to an RRSP

The current law provides for a tax-free transfer of retiring allowances into an RRSP of up to $2 000 for each year in which the employee was covered by a registered pension plan and $3 500 for each year of service with no pension coverage. For 1986 and subsequent years a single limit of $2 000 per year will apply.

The two most common types of retirement allowances are payments for accumulated sick leave credits and retirement gratuities which are usually paid in a lump sum.

4. Maturation of RRSPs prior to age 60

Under existing rules, RRSPs can be matured in the form of a life annuity, term certain annuity to age 90, or a registered retirement income fund between the ages of 60 and 71 only. The minimum age will be removed, effective January 1, 1986.

This eliminates one of the most unreasonable aspects of RRSPs. Why the minister did not remove the maximum age is an interesting question that will be explored in more depth in the chapter on RRSP termination. (See chapter 12.)

5. The "locked in" RRSP

Under existing law, withdrawals from a registered pension plan can be transferred, tax free, to an RRSP or taken into taxable income or transferred to another registered pension plan.

Under the proposed legislation, after two years' participation in a registered pension plan, employees will be entitled to a retirement benefit based on both their own

AND their employer's contributions. This is called "vesting." All employer and employee contributions will be "locked in" once vested and will not be available to the employee until retirement.

However, vested benefits will be portable and employees will have the following choices when leaving an employer before retirement:

(a) Transferring the entire value of the vested pension to a "locked in" RRSP
(b) Transferring the vested pension to the new employer's registered pension plan
(c) Leaving the vested pension with the former employer until retirement
(d) Transferring their own contributions together with interest to a locked in RRSP, while leaving the remaining entitlement with their former employer as a deferred benefit to be available on retirement

These changes will apply only to pensions earned after the legislation becomes effective, January 1, 1987.

Although the budget documents do not speak specifically about locked in RRSPs, it is hoped that transfers between existing locked in RRSPs will be allowed in the same way as transfers between other RRSPs.

6. Excess contributions

Under current law, excess contributions to RRSPs are not deductible. Excess amounts above a threshold of $7 500 are subject to a penalty tax of 1% per month and to full taxation upon withdrawal.

Under the budget proposals, the 1% tax on excess contributions will be maintained but withdrawals of non-deducted excess contributions will be permitted tax-free.

If you contribute more than the maximum allowable amount but less than $7 500, you will be permitted up to two years to withdraw the overcontribution from your own plan or your spouse's plan without tax consequences. However, the timing of the refund is important.

For example, suppose you have net earned income of $20 000. You paid $1 400 into a pension plan with an employer and contributed $5 400 to a registered retirement savings plan.

You may claim the least of —

(a) the amount paid into the RRSP ($5 400),
(b) 20% of your earned income ($4 000) less pension plan contribution of $1 400 ($2 600), or
(c) the $3 500 limit less pension plan contribution of $1 400 ($2 100).

You may deduct $2 100 and claim a refund of excess contributions of $3 300.

To apply for a refund of this excess contribution and for confirmation by Revenue Canada, Taxation of the qualifying amount, you must obtain form T3012, "Application for Refund of Excess Contributions" from your district tax office. The refund may not be obtained before the end of the calendar year in which the contribution was made.

When the qualifying amount that can be refunded has been confirmed by the tax department, form T3012 will be given to your plan issuer who will then refund the amount to you. The amount stated on form T3012 must be included in your income on your income tax return for the year in which you received the refund. However, if you receive the refund before the end of the year in which you received the assessment notice that the deduction was not allowed, or before the end of the following year, you may claim a deduction equal to the amount of the refund included in income.

If you contribute more than $7 500 in a year (other than transfer amounts) and no portion is deductible in the previous year, you must pay a tax of 1% per month while this excess remains in the RRSP. Therefore, when you discover that you have exceeded the $7 500 limit, you should arrange with your plan issuer to have the overcontribution refunded as soon as possible.

No form is needed to obtain this refund, and the Department will not confirm the amount as it can easily be determined by you and your plan issuer.

c. RRSPs ARE REALLY TAX POSTPONEMENTS

A well-chosen registered retirement savings plan is worth serious consideration. However, you should be aware of certain myths created by the advertisers of RRSPs, which often tend to be misleading and, in some cases, downright untruthful. They often refer to contributions to registered retirements savings plans as tax deductions or tax savings. In the vast majority of cases, they are nothing of the sort. They are really tax postponements. In addition, the rates of return on some of the plans are clearly misrepresented.

d. WHY TAX POSTPONEMENT IS ADVANTAGEOUS

There are four distinct advantages to tax postponement:

(a) Plan holders will most likely be in a lower tax bracket and have higher personal income tax exemptions after they retire than when they are working and making contributions.

(b) Your money is accumulating tax-free. The interest, dividends, and capital gains are re-invested in the plan and are not taxed as they would be if the plan were not registered and you had more than $1 000 per year in investment income. For most individuals, the May 23, 1985 budget eliminated tax on capital gains. This means, in this context, that the equity or common stock based RRSPs are less advantageous than they were prior to the budget.

(c) If you are not a member of a registered pension fund, an RRSP is the only way you can take advantage of the $1 000 of tax-free pension income.

(d) Since the contributions are tax deductible, the government is subsidizing the plan at the planholder's marginal tax rate. (Some people call this an interest-free loan.)

e. INCREASED SAVINGS THROUGH RRSPs

The following dramatic example will illustrate the economic advantages of RRSPs. Suppose there are two individuals, each earning enough money to be in the 50%

marginal tax bracket. Suppose, also, that neither is a member of a pension plan and that they can both make a maximum contribution of $7 500 to a retirement savings plan. Each chooses a plan with an average rate of 10% interest each year for 25 years.

Taxpayer A does not register his investment program as an RRSP, so his $7 500 is cut to $2 750 after tax has been deducted. Therefore, he only realizes about 5% after-tax interest on his original $7 500. At this rate of return, he would accumulate a pool of approximately $187 924 over the 25-year period.

Taxpayer B registers her program as a registered retirement savings plan, so her $7 500 annual contribution is tax deductible and no tax is levied on the interest each year.

Compounded over a 25-year period, a pool of savings in excess of $811 358 would be accumulated — 4.32 times greater than the plan that was not registered.

f. DISADVANTAGES VERSUS ADVANTAGES

One disadvantage is that the tax will have to be paid sometime on all of the income generated by the $811 358. The only tax on the $187 924 would be on the income that it generates through whichever option the planholder chooses. It would seem evident that the former would be more advantageous than the latter.

Another disadvantage of placing money in a registered retirement savings plan is inflation. Although dollars invested in RRSPs are subsidized by the government and the interest, dividends and capital gains accumulate tax free, the purchasing power of retirement income dollars will be considerably lower than the dollars that were originally invested.

A third disadvantage of RRSPs is that they may take tax-free investment dollars and turn them into taxable dollars. This occurs when the individual investing in an RRSP has less than $1 000 of investment income in the year the RRSP was purchased.

A fourth disadvantage is that, eventually, all RRSP dollars — accumulated contributions and accumulated investment income — will be taxed at your full marginal rate. Outside the RRSP tax umbrella, only investment income beyond the $1 000 of tax-free investment income is taxed at all. Interest in this category is taxed at the full marginal rate, dividends receive preferential treatment, and by 1990 all Canadian taxpayers will be entitled to the $500 000 capital gains exemption.

A fifth disadvantage is the fact that a more attractive use of available funds may be sitting right under the consumer's nose. Elimination of debts and extra payments on a residential mortgage can often be a wiser use of extra funds than the purchase of an RRSP.

And finally, when the time comes to use the RRSP, you may be too old or too ill to enjoy the money or worse still, you might be dead. If an adequate pension is in the cards, spending the money on your family or on yourself when you are young enough to enjoy it may be a better alternative than an RRSP.

g. TAX REDUCTIONS AND TAX ELIMINATION

As was previously mentioned, in the vast majority of cases, retirement savings plans are tax postponements, not tax savings or tax deductions. However, in some cases, judicious use of the plans can result in dramatic tax reductions and even tax elimination. This may occur when an individual stops working on a permanent basis.

Suppose a married woman earning a high income ceases to work. Suppose that her earned income was $17 000 and her taxable income was $14 000 in her last year of employment, and that she also contributed $700 to the pension plan provided by her employer. Assume also, for the sake of simplicity, that she left on December 31.

She, too, could make contributions to a registered retirement savings plan totalling $2 700. But since neither husband nor wife pays any tax on the first $520 (1986 figure), of the wife's net income, this amount could be withdrawn from the RRSP each year without ever attracting tax. If the woman had been a member of the registered pension plan provided through her employer, the funds in this plan to which she was entitled could be transferred to her RRSP and withdrawn in the same manner.

NOTE: Withdrawals are subject to withholding tax deducted at source which may be claimed as a tax credit for the next year.

Suppose the woman likes the idea of realizing substantial tax savings but does not like the idea of waiting for her money. She should arrange a bank loan with annual payments to be made on January 1 each year. These payments would be made out of the RRSP withdrawal. All this would cost would be the difference between the loan rate and the amount earned by the RRSP. Considering the tax saving this cost would be minimal.

The key phrase in this section is *net income*. Net income is total income earned — employment, old age pension, family allowance, investment and pension income *before* the $1 000 of tax relief, etc. This total is reduced by contributions to Canada Pension Plan, registered pension funds, RRSPs, union dues, tuition fees, child care expenses, carrying charges, moving expenses, etc. The point is that any income the wife receives that reduces her deductibility by her husband is, in effect, taxed at the husband's full marginal rate and, therefore, tax shelters which relate to this issue should be used with caution.

Another alternative might be to leave the money in the RRSP so that, after age 65, the spouse could annuitize the funds and take advantage of the $1 000 of tax-free pension income. This would apply only if the spouse were not at that time being declared as a dependent spouse for tax purposes and the rules were the same at age 65 as they are now.

h. THE BENEFICIARY OF AN RRSP
You may name a spouse, dependent children or grandchildren as beneficiaries to your RRSP. Each child can

receive $5 000 multiplied by the number of years until the child or grandchild becomes 26 years of age. If the child or grandchild is dependent because of mental or physical infirmity, the age and dollar restrictions do not apply.

If the beneficiary is over 71 years of age when the planholder dies, the total amount of money in the RRSP becomes taxable as income in the hands of the beneficiary since you cannot have an RRSP if over the age of 71. So if you have an RRSP and your beneficiary is over 71, you should take immediate steps to terminate the plan.

i. A WORD OF CAUTION

At the time of writing, no changes proposed in the budgets of 1985 and 1986 had become law. Any questions that trouble taxpayers should be referred to Revenue Canada for clarification.

2

FROM WHOM SHOULD YOU PURCHASE A REGISTERED RETIREMENT SAVINGS PLAN?

Literally thousands of plans are available on the market. Banks, credit unions, mutual funds, stockbrokers, trust companies and life insurance companies fight fiercely for the consumer's RRSP dollar. Some people prefer to set up and administer their own RRSP either through a trust company or a stockbroker.

Life insurance RRSPs are so complicated that three chapters are required to explain them. Similarly, mutual funds merit special treatment.

The type of plan and its investment yield are crucial aspects that must be fully explored before deciding which RRSP is the most appropriate for you. A difference of only 1% in the rate of return over a period of years will make a substantial difference in the pool of funds available for the purchase of an annuity or other type of life-time income. (Table #1 shows the rate at which money accumulates over various time periods at different interest rates.)

TABLE #1
AMOUNT TO WHICH A $1 000 ANNUAL INVESTMENT WILL INCREASE OVER TIME AT VARIOUS INTEREST RATES

No. of Years	4%	8%	10%	14%	15%	16%
10	12 486	15 645	17 531	22 044	23 349	24 733
15	20 825	29 324	34 949	49 980	54 717	59 925
20	30 969	49 422	63 002	103 766	117 809	133 840
25	43 312	78 954	108 181	207 332	224 711	289 087
30	58 328	122 345	180 943	406 735	499 955	615 159
35	76 598	186 102	298 126	790 670	1 103 342	1 300 023
40	98 827	279 781	486 851	1 529 904	2 045 946	2 738 469

a. ANALYZING THE RISK

Until recently, the range of investments that qualified for registration as RRSPs was quite restrictive. The May 23, 1985 budget made a significant change in the types of eligible investments.

The budget proposed to permit an RRSP to invest up to 50% of its assets in the shares of Canadian controlled private corporations resident in Canada that are at arm's length from the plan beneficiary. This provision will also apply to registered retirement income funds (RRIFs). (RRIFs are discussed in chapter 12).

To ensure that these investments are limited to genuine arm's length situations, an investment in a corporation by an RRSP of a significant shareholder of the corporation will be considered not to deal at arm's length with the corporation if it is controlled by him or her alone or together with other partners or employees. Within the 50% limit, RRSPs and RRIFs will also be permitted to invest in the same small business investment limited partnerships that pension plans will be allowed to invest in.

The small business investment corporations will be permitted to channel their investments to small businesses and venture enterprises. They will be exempt from tax since they are really a type of channel that transfers investments from registered pension plans and RRSPs to other companies.

The small business investment corporations will be permitted to make investments in shares and unsecured or subordinated debt of small and medium-size Canadian corporations and in units of certain small business investment limited partnerships.

This presents a wider range of RRSP choices but it also is cause for concern. The most important feature of any RRSP should be safety of capital. Private corporations and small business investment corporations as described in the budget are very risky vehicles and, as such, should probably be avoided for RRSP purposes. In addition, shares in these corporations will most likely have a very limited secondary or "after" market. It is quite probable that some people who invest their RRSP dollars in these corporations may find, at retirement, that they cannot turn their hard-earned dollars into a life income. Also, there is cause for concern about how shares in these corporations will be marketed and the role, if any, the provincial securities commission will play in terms of the protection of the public interest.

In summary, at least for a couple of years, stay away from investing RRSP dollars in both private corporations and small business investment corporations.

b. CONVENTIONAL RRSP INVESTMENTS

Most people believe that the more risky an investment, the more likely it is that a greater rate of return will be realized. That is not always the case. In some recent 10-year periods, many low risk fixed income investments substantially out performed higher risk stock market based investments. Part of the reason for this was historically high interest rates coupled with spotty stock market performance.

Even within the stock market based investment range, some plans defined as higher risk by the *Financial Times* did poorly when compared to similar lower risk plans. (This issue is discussed in much more detail in chapters 4 and 5.)

To put the matter of risk in some perspective, I have constructed a risk scale of RRSP investments (see Table #2).

c. TRUST COMPANIES

Trust companies sell the most comprehensive array of registered retirement savings plans of any of the organizations in that business. Their RRSP money is invested in bonds, mortgages, stocks, fixed income securities and, in some cases, a combination of all four. Generally, trust companies levy no loading (acquisition) or withdrawal fees.

They usually charge a small management fee for investments in their stock, bond, and mortgage plans, but their fixed income plans are completely free of any charges. The

TABLE #2
RISK SCALE OF RRSP INVESTMENTS

```
HIGHEST RISK 15 Private corporations
             14 Small business investment corporations
             13
             12
             11
             10 Portfolio of common stocks
              9 Volatile equity fund
              8
              7 Well managed equity fund
              6
              5
              4 Income fund
              3 Mortgage fund
              2
LOWEST RISK   1 Deposits protected by Canada
                Deposit Insurance
```

spread between what the company gets for its money and what the company pays for it provides sufficient profit.

RRSPs have been a large part of trust company business since 1957 and, in my opinion, these companies have more trained, competent and knowledgeable people in the RRSP field than any other group of organizations offering the plans to the public.

Also, trust companies will lend you money to buy a registered retirement savings plan. The interest on these loans is no longer a tax deductible investment expense.

In 1983, a disturbing development occurred involving the fixed or guaranteed RRSPs sold by some trust companies. A typical example was a five-year guaranteed RRSP with a high interest rate where the interest was not compounded at the same rate. It was "dumped" into another pool paying interest at the daily savings rate, which could be one-half the advertised RRSP rate. All this was hidden in the fine print, so beware.

Although this practice is not as widespread as it was in 1983, it is still a problem that some companies insist on perpetrating on an unsuspecting public.

d. BANKS

Generally, bank RRSPs are of a fixed income nature. They often have small acquisition and withdrawal fees and the interest rate they pay is often below that of the trust companies and credit unions, but competition is closing this gap dramatically.

In my opinion, the general level of RRSP expertise in Canadian chartered banks is below that of the trust companies. This is more the case in smaller branches. The reasons are that the banks have not been in the RRSP game as long as the trust companies and RRSPs form a smaller part of the bank's overall business than they do in the trust companies.

There are some advantages to purchasing an RRSP from a bank, particularly in a small community. Bankers don't make their living selling RRSPs, so you won't be harassed or pressured into buying one. Second, like your trust company manager, your banker will probably lend you the money to buy your RRSP.

e. CREDIT UNIONS

Generally, credit unions emphasize fixed income, guaranteed interest plans. Often they have no loading, management or withdrawal fees. Their true rates of return are generally the same as those offered by the trust companies.

Except in very large credit unions, you may have more trouble finding experienced personnel in the RRSP field than you would at a trust company, but they are coming on strong and learning fast.

You may also be able to borrow money from your credit union to buy your RRSP.

Many credit unions may be unwilling to guarantee their rate of return for a period longer than one year. This is because the mortgages in which they invest their funds can usually be paid off at any time and they have no five-year investments to match the mortgages against. Since RRSPs are long term commitments, you might want to think twice about dealing with a credit union.

In addition, the credit union movement has apparently turned a blind eye to the dramatic shift by investors to mutual funds. This will cost them dearly, particularly because of proposed changes in Registered Retirement Income Funds.

f. STOCKBROKERS

Most brokerage houses are deeply involved in the RRSP sales. Generally, their plans can be placed in two categories — mutual funds and self-administered plans.

The mutual funds sold by stockbrokers generally carry a front-end loading charge of 4% to 5% of the amount invested. This is substantially less than the 9% charged by most mutual fund salespeople. However, mutual funds that perform very well can be obtained without any front-end load at all. Such funds are available from banks, trust companies, and the funds themselves.

The second general type is the self-administered plan. The broker provides the securities which can range all the way from guaranteed investment certificates to common stocks. Fees can be as low as $100 per year. (This is in addition to any commission that the broker earns on the buying and selling of the securities in the plan.)

Brokerage houses have been going through a period of mergers in recent years. One result appears to be larger firms staffed by more specialists — a distinct consumer advantage.

The main question about stockbrokers' RRSPs is the quality of their advice, particularly when the self-administered RRSP consists of a portfolio of common stocks. How is the track record of the broker to be measured? Playing the stock market is a good way to have fun, get ulcers, and lose money. When small investors play the stock market they compete against crooks, pros, and people with inside information. Nobody knows how well the crooks and the people with inside information perform, but the track record of the pros who manage equity funds can be obtained from the *Financial Times*.

Over the five-year period ending June 30, 1986, 28.6% did worse than chance. Over the ten-year period ending on the same date, 56.8% did worse than chance. (This study excluded equity funds without tax shelter eligibility.)

Another cause for concern in 1986 appears to be rankings of mutual funds published by stock brokers. Some of these rankings exclude top performing no-load funds. They also ignore front-end loading charges and, as such, are misleading to most consumers.

g. A NOTE OF CAUTION

When you purchase a fixed income type of RRSP from a bank, trust company or credit union, watch both the rate of return and the length of time that the rate is guaranteed. In mid-1986, daily or floating rates were around 5%. Five-year rates exceeded 9%. For some institutions and some vehicles the five-year rates were not compounded at the advertised rate but at the daily rate.

h. WATCH WHAT HAPPENS AT THE OTHER END

Over the past few years I have received a number of complaints from consumers who purchased RRSPs from deposit-taking institutions. The complaints involved people who had retired and wanted to turn their RRSPs into a form of life income. The deposit-taking institutions who were so hot to handle their RRSP money were not interested in what happened when the plan holder turned 71 since they could no longer manage the money. Not only were they not interested, they were downright unhelpful. One trust company forced a planholder to liquidate the plan early because it only allowed withdrawals every two months. So before taking out an RRSP with a deposit-taking institution, find out what they do at the other end!

i. SELF-ADMINISTERED REGISTERED RETIREMENT SAVINGS PLANS

Rather than have someone else administer their retirement savings plans, some individuals prefer to manage their own. This type of arrangement is known as a self-administered registered retirement savings plan.

Self-administered plans may be obtained from both trust companies and brokerage houses. Annual fees for these plans can be as low as $100.

1. Investments

If you have a self-administered plan, you should pay particular attention to the type of investments you choose. A non-qualified investment will result in your having to include the cost of the investment in your income. The following are some of the more common investments considered qualified for purposes of an RRSP:

(a) Money or deposits of money in a Canadian bank, trust company or credit union, other than money where its fair market value is greater than its face value

(b) Certain bonds, debentures and similar obligations guaranteed by the government of Canada, a province, municipality, or Crown corporation

(c) Shares and debt obligations of corporations listed on a prescribed stock exchange in Canada

(d) Certain rights or warrants listed on a prescribed stock exchange in Canada

(e) Guaranteed investment certificates, issued by a Canadian trust company

(f) Certain annuities issued by Canadian corporations

(g) Shares listed on a prescribed stock exchange outside Canada

(h) An annuity bought with plan contributions when converted to a "paying" plan

(i) Shares of the capital stock of a mutual fund corporation

(j) Units of a mutual trust fund

(k) Shares of the capital stock of a public corporation
(l) A mortgage or interest in a mortgage secured by real property located in Canada as long as the mortgagor is not yourself or a person related to you (for exceptions see section g., chapter 3.)
(m) Bonds, debentures or similar obligations issued by certain co-operatives or credit unions
(n) Certain life insurance policies
(o) Shares in certain Canadian-controlled private corporations as proposed by the May 23, 1985 federal budget (see section a. of this chapter).

Some mutual funds in Canada are not considered qualified investments. Shares listed on interim or unlisted boards of prescribed Canadian stock exchanges are qualified investments if they conform to the definition of a public corporation in the Income Tax Act. Shares listed on a prescribed foreign stock exchange are considered qualified investments. The RRSP is subject to the 1% per month tax on excess foreign investments.

2. Non-qualified investments
Any investment not specified as a qualified investment, if acquired after 1971, is non-qualified. Here are some of the more common non-qualified investments:

(a) Employees' options to purchase stock
(b) Gold and silver bars and other precious metals
(c) Shares of almost all private corporations except those proposed in the May 23, 1985 budget (see section a. of this chapter)
(d) Commodity futures, contracts
(e) Listed personal property such as works of art and antiques
(f) Gems and other precious stones
(g) Real estate

Many bonds do not qualify because the issuer is a wholly-owned subsidiary and its shares are not listed on a stock exchange.

If an investment was qualified when acquired by an RRSP but later becomes a non-qualified investment, it is subject to a special tax. If the fair market value of the non-qualified investment has not been included in income by the annuitant, then the RRSP will be subject to a tax of 1% of the fair market value of the property when acquired for each month it is held. A return must be filed and the tax paid within 90 days after the end of the taxation year. If the investment was acquired by the trust before August 25, 1972, the special tax does not apply.

If an RRSP acquires a non-qualified investment, the fair market value of that investment must be added to your income for the tax year the investment is made. Your trustee will send you a T4RSP for this amount. This amount may be included in "earned income" for the purpose of calculating your contribution limit.

In calculating your taxable income for the year in which the non-qualified investment is sold, you will be able to deduct either the amount brought into income or the proceeds of disposition, whichever is less. This deduction, however, reduces the maximum amount you may otherwise deduct for contributions to an RRSP in that particular year. In effect, this amount is considered the same as a contribution. A T4RSP is issued both when the non-qualified investment is acquired and when it is disposed of.

3. Property

Your contributions to an RRSP may be in the form of stocks and bonds rather than cash. Your contribution for tax purposes is the fair market value of the securities at the time of contribution. Be sure to transfer the ownership registration of the securities.

When the security is contributed, you will receive a receipt for its fair market value. This amount is treated as a contribution to your RRSP and becomes an investment of the plan. If any contributed security is a non-qualified investment of the trust, its fair market value must be added to your income for that year.

The contributor must calculate any capital gains or loss on the disposition of property transferred to an RRSP. The loss, if any, on transfer of property to an RRSP after May 25, 1976 is not deductible by the contributor.

If your RRSP acquires property at a price higher than its fair market value, the difference between the cost of acquisition and the fair market value must be included in your income of that year. Similarly, if your RRSP disposes of property below its fair market value, the difference between the proceeds of disposition and the fair market value must be included in your income.

The following are several points that should be kept in mind by people administering their own registered retirement savings plans:

(a) Penalties for making unqualified investments are severe.

(b) Unless the plan has a total dollar value of at least $10 000, the costs can become prohibitive in terms of a percentage of the amount invested.

(c) There are a number of intricate legal points covering the role of the annuitant, the trustee, and beneficiaries that should be very carefully considered before entering into a self-administered plan. It would be wise for anyone considering such a course of action to obtain good trust advice, good investment advice, and good legal advice.

(d) If you have some qualifying securities that, for whatever reason, you do not wish to sell, you might consider placing them in a self-administered RRSP. This would mean that you would not have to raise the cash for your RRSP.

(e) Consider the conflict of interest that could be associated with a self-administered plan where the contributions are a pool of common stocks. The more frequently the stocks are bought and sold, the more money the broker makes. Many knowledgeable stock market observers feel that the best strategy is to buy quality stocks with long-term growth potential as opposed to a constantly churning portfolio.

3

HOW TO TRANSFER
OR CASH IN A PLAN

a. TRANSFERRING ASSETS

The Income Tax Act allows you to defer payment of income tax on certain types of income you may receive by transferring any amount of the qualifying income to an RRSP under which you are the annuitant. There are different types of income that may be transferred to an RRSP as discussed below.

1. Transfer of pension benefits

Pension income may be transferred to registered retirement savings plans in the year received or within 60 days after the end of the year. The following types of pension income may be transferred:

(a) Benefits from the Canada or Quebec Pension Plans

(b) Old age security payments

(c) Superannuation or pension benefits

(d) Income from an annuitized RRSP

The May 23, 1985 budget proposed that tax-free pension transfers would be permitted only up to the amount of an individual's unused contribution room. This provision will apply to the transfer of Canada or Quebec Pension Plan benefits and old age security benefits as well as to benefits received from registered pension plans. To allow transitional relief to individuals now retired or close to retirement, this change will not come into effect until January 1, 1990.

2. Transfer of deferred income

The following types of deferred income may also be transferred to an RRSP in the year received or within 60 days after the end of the year:

(a) Payments from a deferred profit-sharing plan (except annuity payments under a deferred profit-sharing plan)

(b) Amounts received as deferred pay by military personnel

The May 23 budget did not speak to these issues, so it seems relatively safe to assume these old rules will apply.

3. Transfer of retiring allowances

A retiring allowance is an amount that is received upon retirement from an office or employment in recognition of long service, and includes a payment for unused sick leave credits. It also includes any amount received for loss of office or employment, whether or not it was received as payment of damages or under an order or judgment of a competent tribunal.

Unlike pension benefits, you may not transfer the entire amount of a retiring allowance to an RRSP. The amount is now limited to $2 000 for each year of employment plus an additional $1 500 for each year of that employment for which no amount was vested in you in the employer's RPP or DPSP.

The existing limits on tax-free transfers of retiring allowances will be replaced for 1986 and subsequent years by a single limit of $2 000 per year of service. For service prior to 1986, the current limits will continue.

4. Transfer of a refund of premiums under an RRSP

If you receive a refund of premiums under an RRSP as a result of the death of your spouse, you may transfer this amount or any portion of it to an RRSP in your own name.

5. Transfer procedures and general comments

Qualifying income may be transferred only to RRSPs in your own name. Transfers to spousal plans are not permitted.

You may make payments to the RRSP at any time during the year in which you received the qualifying income, or in the first 60 days of the following year. It is not necessary to make a contribution to your RRSP at the time you receive the qualifying income. If you wish, however, you may arrange to have the funds sent directly to the RRSP issuer, and thus avoid having income tax deducted at source.

When you file your income tax return and claim a deduction for a transfer, you must include a designation in your return stating how much you are transferring to an RRSP under each applicable paragraph of the Income Tax Act. Form T2097 has been prepared to assist taxpayers in calculating their maximum RRSP deduction and it contains designation areas that should be used.

If you wish to transfer all or part of one RRSP to another, you should write a letter to the new plan, informing its manager of the desire to transfer. The letter should include full details of the old plan. The issuer of the new plan will then complete the required procedures to comply with the Income Tax Act and arrange for the transfer from the old plan to the new.

b. PARTIAL DE-REGISTRATION

If holders of RRSPs wish to cash in part of their plans, they must take the following steps:

(a) Decide how much they want to cash in.

(b) Subtract the amount they want to cash in from the total amount of the plan.

(c) Transfer the amount in (b) to a new RRSP (usually with the same firm).

(d) Cash in the amount remaining in the old plan.

The amount cashed in becomes taxable income for the calendar year in which it is received and is subject to withholding tax.

c. SPOUSAL PLANS

One of the newer wrinkles in RRSP legislation allows people to contribute all or part of their eligible RRSP contributions to plans owned by their spouses. The overall dollar amount of their contributions remains the same.

The advantage of this type of arrangement is that if one partner in the marriage is in a much lower tax bracket at retirement, the income from the RRSP will be taxed at a lower rate. The disadvantage of contributing to an RRSP for a spouse is that, if the marriage breaks up, there is a possibility that the contributions will be lost forever to the contributor.

Recent provisions allow for the tax-free transfer of RRSP funds between spouses upon marriage breakdown.

If a spouse cashes in an RRSP within three years after the last spousal plan was purchased, the resulting income is taxed as though it were received by the spouse who claimed the original deduction.

Another advantage of the spousal plan is that, after age 65 if the spouse has no other pension income, the first $1 000 of RRSP income is tax-free. This is the amount that a life annuity would generate if the annuity were purchased with about $7 700 in mid-1985.

An interesting spousal RRSP wrinkle arises from the amount of *net* income a spouse can earn before the deduction for the income-earning spouse is impaired. For 1986, this amount was $520.

One way to take advantage of this $520 would be for the income-earning spouse to buy a spousal RRSP that would, in three years, generate enough investment income to equal $520.

d. DEATH OF THE PLANHOLDER

If the annuitant dies before the plan has matured, generally the full value of the property held by the plan will be included in income of the deceased for the year of death unless the plan funds are to pass directly to the spouse or, if there is no spouse at the time of death, to dependent children or grandchildren and qualify as a "refund of premiums."

If the amount is paid to the estate of the annuitant and not directly to a beneficiary, an election may be required to permit the amounts to be treated as paid directly to the specific beneficiary.

If the plan had matured prior to the annuitant's death and the remaining annuity payments under the plan are payable directly to the spouse, these payments will be included in the income of the spouse. The value of annuity payments that are to pass to a non-spouse beneficiary must be computed and included in the income of the deceased for the year of death unless the amounts are paid to dependent children or grandchildren and qualify as a "refund of premiums."

A refund of premiums means any amount paid out of an RRSP to the spouse as a consequence of the annuitant's death prior to the plan's maturity. If the annuitant had no spouse at the time of death, it means amounts paid out of the plan to a dependent child or grandchild (whether death occurred before or after maturity of the plan) subject to certain limitations regarding the amounts paid to such dependants. A spouse may "roll-over" or transfer all or part of a refund of premiums to his or her own RRSP.

e. LEAVING CANADA

If you leave Canada, you do not have to withdraw the funds from your plan. Your RRSP retains its status, and income earned in the plan continues to compound tax free as long as the funds are not withdrawn.

As an emigrant, you have 60 days after the end of the calendar year in which you became a non-resident to make a contribution. To calculate your contribution limit, your "earned income" is part of your income that is taxable in Canada only.

Non-residents are permitted a tax-free transfer from an RRSP to a registered pension plan or an RRSP under which the non-resident is the annuitant.

If you decide to withdraw the funds from your plan, the entire proceeds are subject to 25% non-resident withholding tax. If your plan is left to maturity and converted to an annuity or an RRIF, the periodic payments are subject to a non-resident tax of 25%.

If you reside in a country with which Canada has a tax agreement, and this agreement exempts annuities from taxation, no withholding tax need be deducted from the periodic benefits. This applies only to periodic payments from an annuity. The leaflet, *Canada and its Tax Treaties*, available from your district taxation office, contains more information on tax agreements.

f. WHEN TO MAKE RRSP CONTRIBUTIONS

Most people make their RRSP contributions late in February of each year so they may deduct them from the previous year's income for tax purposes.

However, there is a lot to be said for making the contributions early in the previous year. For example, the contribution for 1986 can be made any time between January 1, 1986 and March 1, 1987. The person who makes the contribution as early as possible picks up an extra 14 months of tax sheltered investment income each year. This can make a substantial difference at retirement. A $1 000 annual contribution for 20 years at 10% average rate of return will amount to $63 002. Investing 14 months early will add another $7 322 to the pool of retirement income.

If you earn more than $1 000 of investment income each year, it is even more important to invest in your RRSP as early as possible. First, you obviously have the funds and, second, investment income outside the RRSP tax shelter is taxable while investment income inside the shelter escapes tax until it is withdrawn.

The only problem with buying an RRSP early in the year is that you may have difficulty estimating your allowable deduction for that year. If this is the case, make a conservative estimate, make the contribution and top it up with an additional contribution when you know exactly what you will be allowed for that particular year.

g. BORROWING FROM YOUR RRSP

Recently, Revenue Canada has relented somewhat from its long-held position that RRSP investments must be at "arm's length" from the planholder. The result is that you can now place a mortgage on your home in a self-administered RRSP. This enables you to raise cash for another investment, pay off debts, buy a vacation home, etc.

In order to do this you should have at least $50 000 in your RRSP and your home must be debt free. You must follow the following procedure:

(a) Transfer all of your RRSP assets to a self-administered plan.

(b) Arrange to have the self-administered plan give you a loan secured by a mortgage on your home.

(c) Ensure that the mortgage is through an NHA approved lender and that the terms are the same as those offered to other borrowers.

(d) Withdraw the funds.

The main advantage to this is that the interest you pay to your RRSP may be higher than you could otherwise earn with a plan with a similar investment risk. You might be able to arrange an open mortgage that will allow you to make weekly or bi-weekly payments and payments on the principal at your convenience. This will substantially reduce the amount of interest you will pay over the life of the mortgage.

However, the costs of an NHA mortgage are high. You will have to pay a mortgage insurance fee of 1% to 1-1/2% of the amount of the mortgage. In addition, you will have to pay legal fees, survey fees, an appraisal fee, mortgage set-up fees, mortgage administration fees, and the self-administered RRSP fee.

A much better alternative might be a straight bank loan if you need the money, or perhaps a non-NHA mortgage through a credit union.

h. BORROWING FOR YOUR RRSP

Prior to 1981, it was common practice to borrow money to purchase RRSPs and write off the interest on the loan as a tax deductible investment expense. This tax break was abolished in 1981.

However, the May 23, 1985 budget has proposed allowing unused RRSP contributions to be carried forward for a maximum period of seven years, beginning in 1987, and some individuals, who fancy themselves both financial advisors *and* RRSP salespeople, have used the new carry-forward proposals to come up with a new and interesting strategy to borrow funds for the purchase of RRSPs and deduct the interest on the loans as an investment expense. Briefly, here is how it works.

Rather than investing in RRSPs each year, the individual borrows money to purchase an investment similar in amount to the maximum RRSP contribution to which the individual is entitled. Mutual funds are keen on the strategy. The investment is NOT registered. This process is carried on for the full seven years and then the total accumulated amount is then placed behind the RRSP tax shelter. Since the money was borrowed for a non-RRSP investment, interest is unquestionably tax deductible. However, there are a number of problems with this strategy.

First, only the unused contributions, not their accumulated value, can go into the RRSP. This may or may not present difficulties, depending on whether or not the individual really wants a maximum amount of funds behind the shelter to purchase some sort of retirement income in the form of a registered retirement income fund or annuity.

Second, the investment gain outside the tax shelter would be subject to income tax. This would be at the full rate if the individual chose an income or interest paying type of investment and the individual was over the $1 000 of tax-free investment income. If the investment was a mutual fund or a pool of common stocks there would be no tax on the capital gain as long as the new limits were not exceeded. Tax would have to be paid on the dividends, if any, that were earned by the investment.

Third, by accumulating unused contributions for seven years, a lower tax refund might be received than if the funds were put into an RRSP each year. For example, the individual might be in a 40% marginal tax bracket. By making an annual contribution to an RRSP, 40% of the amount of the contribution will be returned each year. But by accumulating, say, $14 000 of unused RRSP contributions and deducting them all in one year, the large contribution might reduce the individual to a marginal tax bracket much lower than 40%. This will mean that much less than 40% of the $14 000 will be returned in the form of an income tax refund.

Fourth, since the tax rebate will be returned seven years down the road it must be reduced by a present value factor. A dollar in hand now is much better than a dollar received seven years from now.

All in all, borrowing money for an RRSP type of investment and letting the unused contributions accumulate for seven years is a questionable strategy. It should not be adopted without careful thought. It is a good gimmick for people who sell common stocks and mutual funds and it seems safe to assume that these individuals will tell only one side of the story. Buyer beware!

i. THE WITHHOLDING TAX

When you cash in a registered retirement savings plan the issuer is required to hold back a portion of the plan and remit the amount held back to Revenue Canada. You are entitled to a tax credit for this amount when you file your next tax return. The amounts withheld are as follows:

Not over $5 000 — 10%
Over $5 000 and not over $15 000 — 20%
Over $15 000 — 30%

(The province of Quebec has somewhat different rates.)

4
INTRODUCTION TO MUTUAL FUNDS

Mutual funds are business organizations that invest other people's money in various types of securities, such as bonds, stocks, and mortgages. The total investment of the fund is known as its portfolio. Mutual funds are really glorified investment clubs that hire professional money managers to make their investment decisions for them. Just how professional they are is quite another matter.

The first type of mutual fund in modern capitalist history was known as an investment trust. The first of these trusts was established in Britain in the 1860s. (Incidentally, mutual funds are still referred to as investment trusts in library classification systems and in many book catalogues.)

Investment trusts came to North America in the 1920s, with the formation of the Massachusetts Investors' Trust in 1924; less than a decade later they began in Canada. In 1940, the Canadian Investment Fund and Commonwealth International Corporation were formed.

Tracing the growth of investment trusts, or mutual funds, as they are now known, is somewhat of a catch-as-catch-can exercise. The common yardstick is the net asset value of the funds and, as will be shown later, this is based upon the market value of the portfolio of the fund on a given date. As the market fluctuates, so fluctuates the net asset value of the portfolios.

In any case, the number of dollars invested in mutual funds by Canadians has grown remarkably since 1940 when the combined assets of the Canadian Investment Fund and Commonwealth International Corporation totalled $7.5 million. In the 1950s and 1960s, mutual funds became a very popular investment medium.

In mid-1986, mutual funds that were members of the Investment Funds Institute of Canada had assets of about $15 billion. This represented a $2.6 billion increase in a little over six months. More than 1.2 million Canadians owned shares in mutual funds in mid-1986, up dramatically from 800 000 one year earlier. These substantial numbers explain why mutual funds deserve careful and thoughtful examination in any tax or family finance book.

a. WHY ARE THEY POPULAR?

There are a number of reasons for the growing popularity of the mutual fund as an investment medium. One is simply the fact that people today have more surplus money to invest than they ever had before. Another reason is that many mutual funds, in addition to having a high advertising budget, have a sales staff who actually get out and push the idea of investing in mutual funds. This has resulted in many people, who would otherwise never have done so, using this investment medium. But perhaps the concept of the registered retirement savings plan provided the greatest impetus to the growth of mutual funds from 1957 on.

As was pointed out earlier, a mutual fund is a business organization that invests other people's money in a broad range of securities. The fund, for various reasons, then arbitrarily divides the total net asset value into small portions it calls shares. These shares are usually valued between $5 and $15 and are usually calculated to the third decimal place. So, if the portfolio of a fund on a given day is valued at $1 000 000, and it has sold 100 000 shares, each share will be valued at $10. The value of the shares goes up and down as the value of the portfolio goes up and down. This is the arrangement devised by most mutual funds. The exception is the closed-end investment fund, which will be explained at the end of this chapter.

b. TYPES OF MUTUAL FUNDS

Mutual funds are divided into two broad categories: open-end and closed-end. The most common and best known are the open-end funds, which create a continuous flow of new shares as money flows into the fund.

1. Types of open-end funds

Open-end mutual funds are subdivided into a number of categories, the most widely known being the common stock fund. A brief description of each follows.

(a) Balanced funds

The portfolio of the balanced fund is made up largely of common stocks, but a sprinkling of more stable securities, such as bonds and preferred stocks, is added. The reason for this is that the managers of the balanced funds want to smooth out the peaks and valleys caused in the net asset value of the funds by stock market fluctuations. One of the best known balanced funds is Investors' Mutual, sold by an organization often referred to as Investors Syndicate.

(b) Fully-managed funds

This type of mutual fund operates, as the *Financial Post* Survey of Investment Funds states, "in the light of conditions at the time." Its managers shift the portfolio around from one type of security to another as they see fit. If, for example, a manager felt fairly certain that there would be a general drop in the market, he or she would sell common stocks and buy bonds. If the drop occurred, and the manager felt that it had reached its low point, he or she would probably sell the bonds and buy common stocks again. And, if the market went back up, a healthy profit would be realized for the fund and its shareholders. (The individual mutual fund holder can play this game too, and how to do it will be explained later in the book.) A famous fully-managed fund is Templeton Growth, one of the best performers of all mutual funds available to Canadians.

(c) Specialty funds

This type of mutual fund buys its securities from industries of one particular type or from one particular geographical location. Examples are Canadian Gas and Energy and Canadian South African Gold.

(d) Speculative funds

These funds invest primarily in securities that have a good growth potential. For this reason, they are often called growth funds. Speculative funds often carry a number of convertible securities in their portfolios. Speculative funds often go up and down faster than the stock exchange indexes. An example of a speculative fund is United Venture, sold by United Funds.

(e) Common stock funds

These funds invest almost all their money in common stocks, although not completely in growth stocks, as do the speculative funds. The Royal Bank of Canada sells a well-known common stock mutual fund that it calls Royfund.

(f) Income funds

Income funds invest in corporation bonds, government bonds, and debentures. These funds grow at a slow, stable pace, and their performance has nothing to do with what happens in the stock market.

(g) Mortgage funds

As the name implies, this type of fund invests in mortgages; most mortgage funds are sold by trust companies.

(h) Combined funds

This type of fund is a combination of the other funds sold by an organization such as a trust company.

(i) Guaranteed funds

These funds are sold mostly by trust companies for RRSP purposes. The interest rates are guaranteed for short durations — three to six months.

(j) Money market funds

These relatively new funds invest in a selection of short-term, high-yield financial instruments such as treasury bills. The fund yields tend to run about two percentage points above bank savings accounts. The interest is accrued daily and paid at regular intervals. The funds are particularly attractive to individuals who wish to "park" funds for short periods of time.

(k) Indexed funds
Indexed funds simply invest in a selection of the shares traded on the Toronto Stock Exchange. The funds' goal is to match the performance of the TSE 300. Given the record of the majority of Canadian equity funds, achieving this target would put these funds consistently among the very best performers. Other advantages of indexed funds are the substantial reduction of brokerage commissions and management fees. The Toronto-Dominion Bank is the latest high profile entry into the indexed fund field.

(l) Dividend funds
Recently, some organizations have been marketing mutual funds that have as their objective maximum payment of dividends. These funds are of interest to people who have no debts and who have more than $1000 in annual investment income. Investors can take advantage of the preferential tax treatment without selecting their own portfolio of common stocks.

(m) Gold funds
These funds are invested in the shares of gold mines.

(n) Real estate funds
Real estate funds are invested in various real estate ventures.

(o) Funds not eligible for tax shelters
In its monthly survey, the *Financial Times* lists a number of funds not eligible for tax sheltering. Of these funds, most are common stock-based. In most cases they are not eligible for tax sheltering because a substantial portion of their assets are invested outside of Canada. Many have performed well and merit consideration because they allow the small investor to diversify into foreign markets and

perhaps be protected against a drop in the Canadian market. Perhaps the best known of these funds is Templeton Growth.

2. Closed-end funds

The closed-end funds are a different type of investment medium, resembling a corporation more than an investment club. They do invest other people's money, but they do not create new shares on demand from the public. If anyone wants to buy shares in a closed-end mutual fund, he or she must buy them from another shareholder. Another characteristic of closed-end funds is the extent to which the value of the funds' shares reflect the net asset value of the portfolio. Unlike the open-end funds, the share value of the closed-end fund does not always accurately reflect the net asset value of the portfolio.

5

MUTUAL FUNDS: BENEFITS VERSUS RISKS: SOME COMMON MYTHS DISPELLED

a. ADVANTAGES OF INVESTING IN MUTUAL FUNDS

There are several advantages to investing in mutual funds, although not as many as the mutual fund salespeople would like us to believe. The advantages that can hardly be disputed are diversification, saving time and brokerage fees, and the use of most mutual funds for the purpose of registration as retirement savings plans and deferred profit sharing plans under the appropriate sections of the Income Tax Act. The advantages of diversification and convenience apply to all mutual funds, but other advantages such as long-term growth and professional management apply only to a select few mutual funds.

1. Diversification

The one universal and undisputed advantage of investing in mutual funds, particularly equity funds, is diversification. There is no possible way that the small investor can own a share or part of a share of many large companies except through the purchase of shares in a mutual fund.

To illustrate the scope of the diversification of a few investment dollars, an example is appropriate. The fund chosen for the example is the Canadian Anaesthetists Mutual Accumulating Fund, which is an equity fund. It is historically one of the better managed Canadian equity funds that can be used for an RRSP.

The minimum initial purchase is $500. As of September 27, 1985, the value of one unit was $9.68, so for $500, an individual could have owned 51.65 units and a piece of the action of every one of the securities listed in the portfolio.

If an individual wanted to buy one share of each of the common stocks in the portfolio on September 27, 1985, the total cost excluding brokerage would have amounted to about $1 879. Table #3 illustrates the portfolio. A side benefit to the advantage of diversification is the savings in brokerage fees. If you purchased one share of each of the common stocks in the portfolio, your brokerage charges would be astronomical. But, since mutual funds purchase shares in such large lump sums, brokerage cost per share or per unit is almost insignificant.

2. Convenience

Most people have neither the time nor the expertise to play the stock market for themselves. By purchasing a mutual fund either on a one-time basis or through a periodic investment plan, individual consumers buy not only a mutual fund but *perhaps* professional money management along with it. The cost and quality of this professional management is examined in subsequent sections. But for those immediately interested, the fee varies between somewhat less than one and somewhat more than two percent of the funds under administration. It is collected on an annual basis.

3. Regularity of investing

Many proponents of investing in mutual funds point to regularity of investing as an advantage, and most mutual funds make it possible to do this. Even by investing a small sum of money each year, over a number of years, a significant amount will be accumulated. Regularity of investing is an advantage if, and only if, the investor does not get hooked into a scheme where half of his or her investment during the first year goes, not into the fund, but into a salesperson's pocket.

TABLE #3
PORTFOLIO OF THE
CANADIAN ANAESTHETISTS'
MUTUAL ACCUMULATING FUND
STATEMENT OF INVESTMENT PORTFOLIO
(as of September 27, 1985)

Face amount	Governmental securities	Average cost	Market value
	British Columbia Treasury Bills		
$ 300 000	9.08%, November 13, 1985	$ 293 358	$ 293 358
	Canada Treasury Bills		
400 000	8.83%, December 20, 1985	391 848	391 848
100 000	8.75%, December 27, 1985	97 865	97 865
100 000	9.05%, October 18, 1985	97 793	97 793
700 000	9.34%, October 4, 1985	684 068	684 068
275 000	9.07%, October 25, 1985	268 920	268 920
300 000	9.06%, November 1, 1985	293 373	293 373
100 000	9.08%, November 8, 1985	97 739	97 739
100 000	8.95%, November 29, 1985	97 817	97 817
100 000	9.10%, November 1, 1985	97 925	97 925
100 000	9.47%, March 21, 1986	95 491	95 491
300 000	8.98%, December 6, 1985	293 430	293 430
1 800 000	9.04%, November 15, 1985	1 760 328	1 760 328
400 000	9.02%, December 6, 1985	391 676	391 676
200 000	8.95%, November 22, 1985	195 634	195 634
100 000	10.45%, October 11, 1985	95 515	95 515
	Manitoba Treasury Bills		
100 000	9.05%, October 23, 1985	97 793	97 793
100 000	9.05%, November 13, 1985	97 984	97 984
	New Brunswick Treasury Bills		
150 000	9.07%, October 17, 1985	146 683	146 683
600 000	9.10%, December 5, 1985	587 262	587 262
	Saskatchewan Treasury Bills		
300 000	9.00%, October 30, 1985	293 430	293 430
1 500 000	9.02%, December 4, 1985	1 467 015	1 467 015
	Total governmental securities	7 942 947	7 942 947

Number of shares	Shares		
	Banks		
46 000	The Bank of British Columbia	269 268	223 100
72 000	The Bank of Nova Scotia	573 215	936 000
22 000	Canadian Imperial Bank of Commerce	788 626	797 500
30 000	The Royal Bank of Canada	711 951	911 250
72 000	The Toronto-Dominion Bank	936 864	1 611 000
		3 279 924	4 478 850

TABLE #3 — Continued

Number of shares	Shares	Average cost	Market value
	Communication		
23 500	Baton Broadcasting	422 559	437 689
57 000	Thomson Newspapers Limited —		
	Class A participating convertible	532 000	1 182 750
		954 559	1 620 439
	Financial — trust and loan		
49 000	National Victoria & Grey		
	Trust Company	$ 743 578	$1 004 500
	Financial — other		
51 000	FCA International Ltd.	285 256	949 875
14 000	Power Financial Corporation	386 588	346 500
48 100	Traders Group Limited, Class A	537 579	1 046 175
		1 209 423	2 342 550
	General manufacturing		
33 900	Camco Inc.	381 984	516 975
64 000	CCL Industries Inc., Class B	478 418	1 000 000
23 000	Dofasco Preferred Shares	747 500	756 125
64 000	Innopac Inc.	630 713	896 000
85 000	Magna International Inc., Class A	414 375	1 657 500
		2 652 990	4 826 600
	Management		
26 200	CAE Industries Ltd.	359 193	393 000
88 000	International Thomson		
	Organization	676 816	770 000
		1 036 009	1 163 000
	Merchandising		
37 000	Provigo Inc.	815 480	952 750
	Mining — precious metals		
15 000	Golden Sceptre Resources Ltd.	100 948	133 125
4 200	Lac Minerals Ltd.	67 899	141 225
		168 847	274 350
	Mining — other		
21 100	Falconbridge Ltd.	306 427	377 163
10 000	International Corona Resources	92 250	153 750
19 000	Rio Algom Limited	194 872	427 500
11 100	Tara Exploration & Development	173 290	199 800
		766 839	1 158 213
	Oil and gas		
80 000	Computalog Gearhart	822 243	980 000
93 000	Dome Canada Limited	456 562	697 500
100 500	Dome Petroleum Limited	331 650	279 390
17 000	Imperial Oil Ltd., Class A conv.	646 707	858 500
10 000	Intercity Gas Corporation	110 243	155 000
180 000	Morgan Hydrocarbons	691 200	675 000
14 800	Norcen Energy Resources		
	Limited — ordinary non-voting	197 272	216 450
22 500	Texaco Canada Inc.	403 650	337 500
		3 659 527	4 199 340

46

TABLE #3 — Continued

Number of shares	Shares	Average cost	Market value
	Office equipment		
45 000	Moore Corporation Limited	$ 478 794	$1 102 500
	Pipelines		
38 400	TransCanada Pipelines Limited	418 349	974 400
	Real estate		
35 000	Campeau Corporation	593 901	870 625
	Resources services		
16 500	Atco Limited, Class 1	175 955	162 938
	Technology		
18 500	Northern Telecom Limited	770 862	846 375
	Transportation		
60 000	Laidlaw Transportation	806 387	825 000
	Utilities		
28 000	Bell Canada Enterprises	$ 879 748	$1 158 500
	Holding companies		
52 500	Canada Development Corporation	301 875	249 375
14 000	Canadian Pacific Enterprises	401 450	379 750
		702 920	629 125
	Non-Canadian		
5 500	Federal Express	251 318	338 808
3 500	F.W. Woolworth	233 446	229 380
6 800	Ford Motor Company	140 486	411 908
3 600	International Business Machines	536 423	609 854
7 000	Handleman Company	209 928	204 825
4 000	Imperial Chemical PLC	211 576	199 862
2 200	Kroger Company	136 619	127 994
7 200	M.D.C. Corporation Delaware	140 205	115 811
3 600	McDonalds Corporation	193 384	317 247
2 500	Penwalt Corporation	128 294	127 481
4 300	Schering Plough Corporation	271 854	279 602
1 200	Texas Instruments Corporation	187 916	151 950
1 200	W.W. Grainger Incorporated	49 850	49 281
3 500	Zayre Corporation	113 857	241 358
		2 805 156	3 405 361
	Total shares	22 919 248	31 995 416
	TOTAL INVESTMENT PORTFOLIO	$30 862 195	$ 39 938 363

Note: All securities recorded are common shares unless otherwise designated by a class or preference.

Source: The Canadian Anaesthetists' Mutual Accumulating Fund.

4. Dollar-cost averaging

This is an advantage if the fund holder makes regular investments over a period of years. As the *Financial Post* Survey of Funds points out, "If you buy the same stock at varying prices, and invest the same dollar amount each time, the average cost per share will be less than the average of the prices. This happens because your money will buy more shares when the prices are low than when the prices are high." Again, dollar-cost averaging through some form of regular investment program is an advantage if no absurd loading charge is involved.

This magic of numbers that is known as dollar-cost averaging is best illustrated by example. Again we draw on the annual report of the Canadian Anaesthetists' Fund. Table #4 shows how the unit values have fluctuated over the period 1976 to 1985. Assume that $500 was invested at the end of each period shown in Table #4. The average price of the units over the ten-year period was $6.79 and the average cost per share was $5.89 ($500.00 ÷ 847.80 shares).

TABLE #4
DOLLAR COST AVERAGING

Year	Unit Value of Fund	Number of shares purchased by $500
1976	$3.50	142.86
1977	$3.65	136.99
1978	$4.70	122.85
1979	$6.79	73.64
1980	$8.98	55.68
1981	$7.22	69.25
1982	$6.67	74.96
1983	$8.25	60.68
1984	$8.44	59.24
1985	$9.68	51.65

Source: The Canadian Anaesthetists' Mutual Accumulating Fund.

b. THE MYTH OF "PROFESSIONAL MANAGEMENT"

One of the claims made by mutual funds and their sales-people is that the funds are managed by competent and highly-paid professionals. Therefore, the argument goes, those who invest in the funds will receive a very good return on their money. All this is accompanied by flashy graphs, with the investment performance represented by jagged lines soaring upward to the right. This professional management argument is not nearly as neat as many funds make it sound. It is true that some mutual funds are very well-managed and have a history of very good investment performance. However, some have been very badly managed and, as we shall soon see, professional management is not a universal advantage when investing in mutual funds. It is a factor that deserves the most rigorous analysis.

In order to run a quick check on the ability of Canadian equity fund managers I obtained a copy of the July 21, 1986 issue of the *Financial Times*. Over the five-year period ending June 30, 1986, 28.6% of the funds did worse than chance. Over the ten-year period ending on the same date, 56.8% did worse than chance. In fact these percentages are really too high for two reasons. First, loading charges were not taken into consideration and second, the funds tend to do better in rising markets than in stable or declining markets. In recent years, markets have been rising steadily.

The conclusion that must be drawn from all this information about mutual funds is obvious. Only some mutual funds have performed better than a number of random selections of common stocks. This means that professional management is an advantage when investing in some mutual funds, and some funds only. Exactly which ones will be discussed in chapter 8.

The important point is that the performance of any mutual fund depends upon the skill of the management as measured by the history of the fund. Loading charges are merely a price that consumers must pay if they choose to purchase shares in a mutual fund that is distributed by a salesperson, or, some cases, a stockbroker.

6
HOW TO MEASURE THE PERFORMANCE OF EQUITY FUNDS

There are a number of widely-used mathematical measures of mutual fund performance. Among the most common are the arithmetic mean and standard deviation. Some firms, whose business it is to evaluate investment management performance, employ a number of other advanced statistical yardsticks, but they appear to be complicated overkill. Volleys of Greek letters, reams of computer printouts, and batteries of correlation coefficients serve only to dazzle the client and justify (?) huge consulting bills. Average annual growth and standard deviation tell just about everything anybody needs to know about mutual fund performance.

However, average annual growth or average annual compound growth is a mathematical yardstick and should only be used to compare the performance of one mutual fund with others. Unfortunately, it is being widely used to promote certain funds. The problem is that average annual growth is always a bigger number than the actual yield in each of the years in the time period. Therefore, the use of average annual growth figures gives a highly inflated picture of how the fund actually performed. In addition, it ignores loading charges.

a. THE ARITHMETIC MEAN
The arithmetic mean is the most commonly used measure of mutual fund performance, yet it is the crudest and least reliable way of measuring performance. The term "arithmetic mean" is the expression statisticians use when they are discussing the concept laypeople refer to as the average. It is calculated by dividing the appreciation in value of

a mutual fund share over a given time period by the number of years in the time period.

Why is the arithmetic mean one of the crudest and least reliable of all statistical measuring devices? The reason for this is that it fails to account for extreme fluctuations in the annual performances. Since wild fluctuations are common characteristics of the performance of some mutual funds, the arithmetic mean should be used with extreme care in the assessment of mutual fund performance, if it is used at all. However, it is an indispensable springboard that must be used in the calculation of other measures of mutal fund performance, such as standard deviation.

Let us look at the performance of two well-known funds, over a 10-year span. We'll call them Funds A and B (see Table #5).

Fortunately, the average annual increase in net asset value for both of these funds is almost the same — 4.4% for Fund A and 4.6% for Fund B. In addition, both are no-load funds.

TABLE #5
ANNUAL INCREASE IN NET ASSET VALUE
PER SHARE FOR TWO SELECTED MUTUAL FUNDS
FOR A 10-YEAR PERIOD

Fund	1	2	3	4	5	6	7	8	9	10
Fund A	+16	-24	-8	+21	+14	-3	-1	+12	+19	-2
Fund B	+24	-24	-13	+27	+7	-1	-1	+22	+13	-8

A quick glance at Table #5 will make the major drawback of the arithmetic mean quite obvious. Although both funds have almost the same average annual increase in net asset value per share, the swings in the annual performances are much greater for Fund B than Fund A. (Other things being equal, this makes the Fund A plan a better buy.)

b. STANDARD DEVIATION

Perhaps the most widely accepted statistical device that is used in the measurement of variability is the standard deviation. Its strong point is that it compares each item in the distribution of numbers with a standard. That standard is the arithmetic mean. So, obviously, the first step in the calculation of the standard deviation is the arithmetic mean. This was done earlier in the chapter for both Fund A and Fund B.

At this point, it is necessary to define some of the terms and symbols used in the calculation of standard deviation. As with most elite academic groups, statisticians like to confuse people with strange jargon and hieroglyphics. The hieroglyphics they have chosen originate in the Greek alphabet. Only five characters require explanation as far as standard deviation are concerned. They are x, $\bar{x}$, ξ, η and σ.

x is the symbol that refers to each item in the group of numbers for which a standard deviation is being calculated (in this case, the annual change in the net asset value per share of a mutual fund). The group of numbers is called the distribution, and the small letter "n" from the English alphabet refers to the number of items in the distribution. In this case, $\bar{x}$ is the expression that is used for the average or arithmetic mean of these numbers. ξ is the character that denotes the expression "sum of." σ is the lower case Greek letter ξ (sigma) used by statisticians in reference to standard deviation. Therefore, we can express the arithmetic mean with the following Greek letter formula:

$$\bar{x} = \frac{\xi x}{\eta}$$

Now we are ready to proceed with the calculation of the standard deviation for the annual performance of the Fund A. This is done by performing the following operations:

(a) Calculate the arithmetic mean of the performances over the 10-year period.

(b) Subtract the arithmetic mean from each of the items in the distribution.

(c) Square each of the results in step (b). (This gets rid of the negative numbers.)

(d) Add all the squares calculated in step (c).

(e) Divide the answer obtained in step (d) by the number of items in the distribution. (In this case, 10.)

(f) Take the square root of the answer obtained in step (e).

In formula and tabular form, it will look as follows:

$$\sigma = \sqrt{\frac{(X - \overline{X})^2}{\eta}}$$

Plugging the data into the formula, we arrive at a standard deviation of 13.6 for Fund A as shown in Table #6 and, by using the same method, 16.1 for Fund B. A high standard deviation shows a high variability and high variability (or volatility as it is called in the trade) is a bad thing. Therefore, other things being equal, which they really are, Fund A is a better buy than Fund B.

TABLE #6
PERCENTAGE CHANGE OVER PREVIOUS YEAR

Year	X	$X - \overline{X}$	$X - \overline{X}^2$
1	+16	+11.6	134.56
2	-24	-28.4	806.56
3	-8	-12.4	153.76
4	+21	+16.6	275.56
5	+14	+9.6	92.16
6	-3	-7.4	54.76
7	-1	-3.4	11.56
8	+12	7.6	57.76
9	+9	+14.6	213.16
10	-2	-6.4	40.96
			1 840.80

1840.80 ÷ 10 = 184.08

$\sqrt{184.08}$ = 13.6

53

c. THE FINANCIAL POST

The *Financial Post* publishes a quarterly performance survey of most Canadian mutual funds. Late January, April, July and October are the times when the survey appears. The survey shows one, three, five and ten-year performance histories of the funds. They are categorized by type and maximum sales charge, tax shelter eligibility, size of the fund and its change in total net assets from the previous year are also indicated. There is no indication of the risk level of the equity funds.

Unlike its rival, the *Financial Times*, the *Financial Post* also includes life insurance equity funds in its survey but does not indicate the sales charges for these funds.

d. THE FINANCIAL TIMES

The *Financial Times* publishes a comprehensive monthly survey of a large number of Canadian mutual funds. In June, 1985, the survey was expanded to provide readers with even more information. Data are now provided on net asset value per share, the percentage of the portfolio invested in foreign securities, total assets of each fund, recent dividends paid, tax shelter eligibility, maximum sales charge and the percentage change over one and three-month periods as well as the traditional one, three, five and ten-year periods.

The *Financial Times* divides equity funds into three risk categories: high, intermediate, and low variability. Each of these three groupings is further subdivided into those funds that are eligible for tax sheltering and those that are not.

As of the June, 1985 survey, real estate and dividend income funds are also listed and categorized.

The *Financial Times* monthly survey of the funds is the most frequently published and the most comprehensive document on the subject in the Canadian public press. A subscription to this newspaper is a small price to pay for anyone interested in either mutual funds or the broader subject of RRSPs.

e. CONCLUSION

Almost all of the decision-making information on the selection of a mutual fund is historical. The question is often asked, particularly by representatives of the poor performers: "How do you know that past performance is really an indication of what will happen in the future?"

The answer can be broken into two sections: First, the funds that have performed well in the past tend to perform well in the future. Just look at any number of studies of mutual fund performance that end in different time periods. Second, if a fund is a consistent performer, as measured by a low standard deviation, this mathematical characteristic will, in all probability, ensure that the trend will continue and that it will perform well in the future.

7

THE COST OF BUYING IN
AND SELLING OUT:
MORE MYTHS DISPELLED

a. LOADING CHARGES

The question of cost is one of the hottest items in any discussion involving mutual funds. Loading charges are the sums that are skimmed off the top of investments in mutual fund shares. This skim-off is used to pay for salespeople's or brokers' commissions and related expenses. For this reason, mutual funds that distribute their shares in this manner are referred to as "load funds."

Funds that do not levy loading charges are referred to as "no-load funds." Mutual funds tend to try to avoid the term "loading charge" because it has acquired an unpleasant connotation, particularly in the United States. So they prefer the more innocuous expression "acquisition charge."

Loading charges are skimmed off mutual fund investments in two ways. The first is very simple: a straight percentage (usually around 9%) of the sum that is invested. This is known as a level-load. The second type of loading charge applies to the investment programs where the customers sign an agreement to make a monthly investment in a mutual fund, usually for a period of five years. In this case, a large percentage of the contributions during the first year goes, not into the fund, but into the salespeople's pockets. This kind of arrangement is known as a front-end load.

1. Level-load

The amount of a level-load is computed in a number of ways. The mutual funds like to describe the loading charge in terms of the smallest possible number. To do this, they express the charge as a percentage of the total amount subscribed by the investor. If the total amount subscribed is $1 000 and the salesperson gets $90, the fund says the loading charge is 9%. However, only $910 is actually invested in the fund. Expressed as a percentage of the actual investment, the $90 is 9.89%. It is a small point, perhaps, but it is made in almost every respectable book and essay on mutual funds, and it would be unwise not to mention it here.

Many Canadian newspapers carry mutual fund listings based on information provided by the Investment Funds Institute of Canada. The funds that have no loading charges are designated by the letter "n." The funds that have loading charges have no indication as to the maximum or any other amount charged. The listings are far from complete and most consumers would be well advised to refer either to the *Financial Post* or the *Financial Times*.

2. Front-end loads and investment contracts

As was previously stated, a front-end-load is an arrangement usually associated with an investment contract requiring a certain number of monthly investments. A large portion of the first year's contributions are used to pay sales commissions and related expenses. These plans usually involve small initial payments and small monthly payments. Up to 50% of the payments in the first year of the contract are used to pay sales commissions. These amounts are permanently forfeited by the purchaser. (It should be pointed out that people who sign these contracts are under no legal obligation to complete them. But, if they cash in their fund, they lose heavily. The sooner they cash in, the more they lose.)

In defence of the front-end-load and the investments contract, the mutual funds and their salespeople resort to two arguments: the forced saving argument and the convenience argument.

3. Negotiable sales charges

A recent development in the area of mutual fund sales has been the aggressive entry into this market by brokerage houses, particulary around RRSP time.

These firms appear to have discovered mutual funds for a couple of reasons. They may have been losing RRSP business to some of the funds and salespeople who have been very pushy with their sales pitches. And they may have been missing a whole segment of the investing market. Many people like the idea of investing in the stock market but never jump in because of high brokerage costs, because the purchase of a few stocks is perceived to be too risky or because they have only a small amount of money to invest. So they just buy mutual funds.

The most significant aspect of the entry of brokerage houses into the mutual fund market has been the effect on sales charges. The mutual fund salespeople usually charge 9% of the amount invested. Exactly the same funds can be purchased from a brokerage house for only a 5% sales charge. If the amount being invested is very large, the sales commission can be negotiated down to as low as 1%. This is not generally known among consumers and mutual fund sales representatives would very much like to keep things that way.

In any case, this discussion is somewhat academic because not only is there no need to buy mutual funds from a salesperson, there is no need to buy them from a stockbroker either. In fact, both should be avoided because there are many excellent no-load funds available from many different organizations.

The issue of questionable sales practices by mutual fund salespeople and stockbrokers is examined in detail in the next chapter.

b. MANAGEMENT FEES

In addition to front-end loading charges, sales charges, or acquisition fees, there are other charges associated with the purchase of mutual funds.

Some funds have loading charges because that is the way they have chosen to sell their product. Salespeople have to be paid.

All mutual funds have management fees of one sort or another. Income and guaranteed funds use the difference between what they pay and what they receive as their fee.

Equity funds typically charge their fee by deducting their costs from the dividends paid to the unit holders of the fund. The funds receive dividends from the companies whose shares they hold. And that is why dividends to unit holders of mutual funds seem so low.

The funds have to charge a management fee because they have costs that must be paid. Investment counsel fees; legal, audit and trustee funds; office expenses, brokerage fees, and advertising are some of the legitimate unavoidable costs.

The amount of the management fee depends on a number of factors such as how much the fund pays its investment counsel, how actively the fund buys and sells securities and how extensively it advertises. In addition, the size of the fund has some bearing on the size of the management fee. Some of the expenses are relatively constant regardless of the size of the fund. This means that the bigger the fund, other things being equal, the smaller the management fee.

Management fees are usually referred to as an "expense ratio." For the year ending September 27, 1985, this ratio was 0.81% of assets for the Canadian Anaesthetists' Fund. For the year ending December 31, 1985, the ratio was 1.89% and 1.54% for Royfund and AGF Special respectively. For the same year ending April 30, 1985, the ratio was 0.77% for Templeton Growth.

Since the *Financial Times* data on fund performance take management fees into account, these fees should be ignored when selecting a fund. The differences are, for the most part, insignificant.

The issue of management fees is examined further in chapter 8.

c. THE MYTH OF THE FORCED SAVINGS ARGUMENT

This is an old argument that the life insurance industry has also been using for years. The argument turns on the premise that most people, left to their own devices, will not save and will not stick to a regular investment program. Therefore, the life insurance and mutual fund industries should become big brothers and do the saving for the ignorant and irresponsible masses who cannot do it for themselves (all for a hefty fee, of course).

The argument is invalid for two reasons. First of all, there is demonstrable evidence that a large percentage of the investment contracts are not completed. In the United States, the figure quoted by the Security and Exchange Commission is 20%.

In addition, there is ample evidence to show that people do, in fact, save their money. The dramatic increase in the amount of money invested in no-load and level-load mutual funds is but one example. The number of small savings accounts in banks and the amount of money in them has been rising steadily over the years. Deposit accounts in trust companies and credit unions have been rising steadily. The sale of Canada Savings Bonds, guaranteed investment certificates, corporate bonds and investment in common stocks has also been on the increase. The amount of money accumulating in company pension plans has been going up at an explosive rate.

On top of all this, any valid definition of the term "saving" would have to include investments in land, accumulation of equity in homes and other income properties, summer cottages, antiques, and "objets d'art," as well as any useful consumer durable with a resale value reasonably related to its cost. So who says Canadians will not save unless they buy front-end load investment contracts?

The convenience argument used by some mutual fund salespeople should also be examined. It goes something like this: "You do not have a large lump sum to invest, so just sign the document that authorizes our firm to make monthly deductions from your bank account over the next five years or so." There is no doubt that this is a convenient and relatively painless way to invest money in a mutual fund. But the rub is that such a large percentage goes, not into investment, but into the salespeople's pocket.

There are two ways the consumer can conveniently and painlessly invest in a mutual fund on this installment basis and still avoid the big front-end loading charge. One way is to get involved in some sort of a capital accumulation plan, and the other is to borrow a lump sum, invest the money in the mutual fund, and pay back the loan in periodic installments that fits your budget.

d. LOADING CHARGES AND MUTUAL FUND PERFORMANCE

One of the misconceptions that many consumers have about mutual funds is that the funds with loading charges perform better. If you arrive at this conclusion, it would not be surprising because of ideas implanted by salespeople. There are absolutely no grounds for such a conclusion. Unfortunately, it is possible to twist statistics to lead the unwary to believe that load funds perform better than no-load funds.

The listings of mutual fund historical performances appear regularly in both the *Financial Times* and the *Financial Post*. These listings do not take front-end loading charges into account for two reasons. First, the charges vary with the amount of money invested. The more money invested, the lower the loading charge. Second, the charges are often negotiable with some sales organizations charging almost half what others want for the same fund.

But this does not stop some fund salespeople from quoting performance figures that assume that no loading charges exist. This is one of the questionable sales tactics that is discussed in more detail in chapter 8. It is also a good reason to avoid both mutual fund salespeople and stockbrokers when buying a fund.

e. CAPITAL ACCUMULATION PLANS

One of the mutual funds that provides the service of a capital accumulation plan is the Canadian Anaesthetists' Fund. The individual makes contributions of a fixed amount on a monthly basis to a special account with the fund. When the contributions build up to the minimum initial investment required by the fund, the amount in the special account is transferred to the fund. The difference, of course, is that no large front-end loading charges are deducted from the monthly installments. If the fund has a level-load, then this charge is deducted when the lump sum goes into the fund.

f. CAPITAL WITHDRAWAL PLANS

The mirror image of the capital accumulation plan is the capital withdrawal plan. It appeals to many people who have accumulated large amounts of funds outside their RRSPs. When these people retire they transfer their funds to an equity-based mutual fund and make systematic withdrawals from the plan. Many funds have earned in excess of 15% per year over a long time period. If these funds perform in the future as they have in the past, individuals could make an annual withdrawal of 15% of their funds and never touch the accumulated capital. Since capital gains are becoming virtually tax-free and the withdrawal is, in effect, a capital gain, the money comes out tax-free.

If this sounds almost too attractive, maybe it is. There are a number of possible drawbacks to this strategy, among them are the following:

(a) The investment is totally at risk and people who are approaching retirement are usually uncomfortable with risk.

(b) The funds are not protected by deposit insurance.

(c) Sometimes the stock market goes for a tumble and substantial losses, at least on paper, are incurred.

(d) One must choose which fund or funds to use. A good strategy might be several no-load funds including perhaps a foreign fund and an American fund.

No consumer should try this strategy without thought or solely on the advice of a mutual fund salesperson.

g. BORROWING MONEY TO INVEST IN A MUTUAL FUND

Borrowing money to invest in a mutual fund is an even better arrangement than the capital accumulation plan. There are several reasons for this. First, the money goes right into the fund and starts to work immediately instead of sitting around in an account not drawing any interest. Second, it really is a forced saving device. The bank or lending institution that advances the money will not let the matter drop if payments are not made regularly.

In addition, non-payment of the loan will destroy a good credit rating very quickly. Purchasers of front-end investment contracts can stop their payments any time they want to. If they want to cash in their plans, they can do so, but will lose their shirts.

Those who go the bank loan route only lose the level-load (if any) if they cash in their plans. In addition, they pocket any capital accumulation (or absorb capital reduction) of the plan that has occurred between the time of purchase and the time of cashing in. They can deduct interest on the loan for tax purposes unless the mutual fund is used for RRSP purposes, then the interest does not qualify as a tax deductible investment expense.

Another advantage of borrowing to invest in a mutual fund is that the lending institution may take the investment in the fund as collateral, thus reducing the interest rate. This situation is quite common when the deal is made with a trust company and the mutual fund is purchased from the same trust company.

Recently a friend of mine was approached by a mutual fund salesperson with quite an interesting pitch. The salesperson wanted my friend to borrow $100 000 from the bank and use the money to buy shares in a selection of mutual funds. The shares were to be used as collateral for the loan which was to be arranged at prime plus 1%. The interest would, of course, be tax deductible. The capital appreciation of the fund was to be used to pay the interest on the loan and any remaining balance used to reduce the principal. A number of years down the road the loan would be repaid and my friend would have a very tidy nest egg. It sounded almost too good to be true and when capital gains became virutally tax-free it sounded even better.

But, like all things that sound too good to be true there are some potential catches. First, the salesperson who presented himself not as a salesperson but as a financial planner, only recommended load funds. The scheme was presented totally on what had happened in the past to both interest rates and fund performance. But what would happen if interest rates ever exceeded the capital appreciation of the funds? That possibility was never discussed in the sales pitch.

It has also been brought to my attention that this proposal has been presented to individuals with large debts and mortgages which clearly should be paid off before such a strategy is even considered.

By mid-1986 this problem had reached such alarming proportions that the Investment Fund Institute of Canada and the Ontario Securities Commission combined to issue a warning about it. Unfortunately, neither body has the power to stop it.

h. MUTUAL FUNDS AND THE FEDERAL BUDGET

With the virtual abolition of the capital gains tax as proposed in the May, 1985 budget every equity based mutual fund in Canada will have to rethink its marketing strategies. With no capital gains tax, the equity funds are, by definition, better investments than they were before May 23, 1985. The extra risks associated in the past with equities are made more acceptable by virtue of the fact that, for most investors, the only tax on their investment gain will be on dividends. Mutual fund dividends tend to be small and are usually given the preferential tax treatment accorded to ordinary dividends paid by Canadian corporations.

On the other hand, when equity funds are placed inside the RRSP tax shelters, all of their investment gains are eventually treated as if they were interest. The zero tax on capital gains and preferential treatment of dividends is lost. Many mutual funds promote heavily around RRSP time and this promotion will undoubtedly increase dramatically in 1986 and subsequent years as RRSP contribution limits rise, particularly for many thousands of high-income Canadians.

Perhaps the wisest mutual fund RRSP strategy is to place interest bearing investments inside the RRSP tax shelter and equity investments outside. But this wisdom will almost certainly be missing from mutual fund propaganda that blots the landscape in January and February of every year.

i. GETTING OUT OF YOUR RRSP TAX FREE

One of the most alarming developments in the field of personal finance began to occur early in 1986. Seminars were being advertised in the national press that purported to show people how to get out of their RRSPs "tax free." This seemed almost too good to be true.

I attended one of those seminars and here is how the pitch worked. Individuals were advised to borrow a substantial amount of money and invest it in mutual funds. They were advised to withdraw an amount of money from their RRSPs equal to the amount of one year's interest on the loan. The loan interest was a tax deductible investment expense to be offset by the RRSP withdrawal, which was taxable. However, no mention was made of the predicament that would result if interest rates went up and fund performance went down. Both happen regularly, and sometimes simultaneously. Nor was any mention made of costs that would be incurred if the loan had to be secured by a mortgage on a personal residence, as it often is. Also, nothing was said about the front-end load that was associated with the recommended fund.

8

GOOD AND BAD PLANS: HOW TO CHOOSE

a. GUARANTEED PLANS

RRSPs that pay a guaranteed rate of interest are attractive to many people: those who do not understand the other types of plans and those who are afraid of any type of risk. People who are approaching retirement should be thinking of buying guaranteed RRSPs and also they should be thinking of switching other RRSPs to guaranteed plans.

This type of RRSP is sold by almost every institution in the business. Most guaranteed plans are sold by banks, credit unions and trust companies. The rates are usually linked to the prevailing level of interest rates and guaranteed for periods of three months to five years.

The followng are some points to remember when buying a guaranteed RRSP:

(a) Watch out for acquisition and/or withdrawal fees. These charges, even though they seem small, can dramatically affect the rate of return.

(b) Watch the length of time the interest rate is guaranteed. Usually a five-year guarantee is best.

(c) Watch how the interest rate is calculated. Interest compounded semi-annually is better than interest compounded annually. Monthly compounding is better still. For example, 8-1/2% compounded semi-annually results in an annual return of 8.68%.

(d) Watch how the interest is compounded. Some companies pay much less on the interest than the rate for the plan itself.

A general rule is that credit unions and trust companies sell similar guaranteed plans that yield interest rates that are about the same as those of the chartered banks. Life insurance companies also sell guaranteed plans called single premium annuities. They are described in chapter 11. Don't buy them if they carry any loading or acquisition fees or if the rates of return are lower than those paid by banks and trust companies.

Table #7 shows the historic performance of a number of guaranteed plans that are eligible for registration as RRSPs. (**Note:** These rates of return do not include withdrawal fees if any are charged.)

TABLE #7
AVERAGE ANNUAL COMPOUND RATES OF RETURN FOR GUARANTEED RRSPs FOR THE PERIOD ENDING JUNE 30, 1986

AVERAGE ANNUAL COMPOUND RATE OF RETURN				
Company	1 yr.	3 yr.	5 yr.	10 yr.
Canada Trust	3.2%	6.4%	8.2%	9.2%
Investors'	8.0	8.8	10.6	—
Montreal Trust	7.0	7.7	9.9	10.0
Royal Trust	7.0	7.8	8.9	9.5
Scotia Bank	8.7	8.8	10.6	10.4

Note: No acquisition fees except for Investors (8.5%).

Source: *Financial Times*, July 21, 1986.

b. MORTGAGE PLANS

For many people, mortgage-based RRSPs have become a popular choice. They are slightly more risky than guaranteed plans and have outperformed them.

Table #8 shows the average annual compound rate of return for mortgage RRSP funds for several time periods ending June 30, 1986.

TABLE #8
AVERAGE ANNUAL COMPOUND RATE OF RETURN
FOR MORTGAGE RRSP FUNDS
FOR THE PERIOD ENDING JUNE 30, 1986

AVERAGE ANNUAL COMPOUND RATE OF RETURN				
Company	1 yr.	3 yr.	5 yr.	10 yr.
Canada Trust	11.0%	11.9%	14.7%	11.6%
First Canadian	11.4	12.6	15.4	11.8
Guaranty Trust	8.3	10.1	13.4	11.1
Montreal Trust	10.6	11.4	14.1	11.3
Royal Trust "M"	11.3	12.2	15.2	12.0

Note: No acquisition fees.

Source: *Financial Times*, July 21, 1986.

c. INCOME FUNDS

Next on the risk scale come the income funds. The managers of these funds invest your money in bonds, debentures and some preferred shares. These funds are available from most trust companies, banks, and some other financial institutions. Table #9 shows the performance data for a number of these funds.

TABLE #9
AVERAGE ANNUAL COMPOUND RATE OF RETURN
FOR INCOME RRSP FUNDS
FOR THE PERIOD ENDING JUNE 30, 1986

AVERAGE ANNUAL COMPOUND RATE OF RETURN				
Company	1 yr.	3 yr.	5 yr.	10 yr.
Canada Trust	16.8%	16.4%	17.9%	11.8%
Dynamic Income	14.1	14.7	17.0	—
Guaranty Trust	16.1	13.8	17.3	11.2
Montreal Trust	17.9	14.3	18.6	11.5
Royal Trust "B"	16.5	15.3	18.3	11.9
Royfund Income	15.7	13.1	14.2	11.2

Note: No acquisition fees.

Source: *Financial Times*, July 21, 1986.

From time to time, income funds have been known to have drops in the unit values of their shares. The reason for this is the inverse relationship between interest rates and the value of the shares in these funds — as interest rates go up, the share values fall and vice versa. The best way to explain this phenomenon is by example. Suppose, last year, you purchased a $1 000 corporate bond yielding 10% to maturity. If the general level of interest rates went up to 11% and you wanted to sell your bond, you would have to sell it for a price that would yield 11% to the person who bought it. You could get about $910 for it. Similarly, if the general level of interest rates went down to 9%, you could sell your bond for a premium perhaps $1 100. This is what causes the erratic behavior in the unit values of income funds, and it is what has caused the low one-year returns on some mortgage and income funds.

If you are thinking about buying an income fund, deal with a well-known organization that does not levy loading charges and also, beware of new funds with small port-folios. In other words, stick with a trust company.

d. EQUITY FUNDS

It's now 17 years since I first became interested in this topic. Then the stock market was booming. Common stock RRSPs were being peddled on a "look how we did last week" basis. And, as 1968 turned into 1969, thousands of Canadians fell into the stock trap. As we all know, the market collapsed in May of 1969 and millions of dollars were lost by thousands of innocent and helpless people. Some rode out the storm and the value of their equity funds is back to where it started or in some cases a little higher.

Table #10 shows the track records for 11 equity-based mutual funds that can be registered as RRSPs. The five trust company funds are widely available across Canada. Royfund is distributed by the Royal Bank of Canada and can be purchased at any of its branches. The following is the address of the Canadian Anaesthetists' Fund, one of the top performers.

Canadian Anaesthetists' Mutual Accumulating Fund
Suite 901
94 Cumberland Street
Toronto, Ontario
M5R 1A3

TABLE #10
AVERAGE ANNUAL COMPOUND RATE OF RETURN
FOR EQUITY RRSP FUNDS
FOR THE PERIOD ENDING JUNE 30, 1986

AVERAGE ANNUAL COMPOUND RATE OF RETURN					
Company	Maximum sales charge	1 yr.	3 yr.	5 yr.	10 yr.
Associate Investors	Nil	15.0%	17.0%	14.2%	17.3%
Canada Trust	Nil	18.4	11.5	10.0	14.9
Canadian Anaesthetists	Nil	21.7	14.7	12.4	19.4
Dynamic	Nil	15.2	9.8	8.6	17.6
Guaranty Trust	Nil	24.8	17.9	17.4	19.5
Industrial Growth	9.0%	16.4	15.0	17.5	19.5
Investors Retirement	8.5%	13.6	11.4	9.8	13.7
Montreal Trust	Nil	17.7	10.0	9.7	14.0
Royal Trust "C"	Nil	11.3	8.2	8.4	13.4
Royfund	Nil	34.9	21.8	14.3	19.2
United Accumulative	9.0%	22.3	21.4	14.4	18.8
T.S.E. 300		17.4	11.7	9.6	16.0

Source: *Financial Times*, July 21, 1986.

Table #11 shows the performance histories of some of the best known foreign mutual funds. None of these funds is eligible for tax shelter purposes. This table has been included because many people who like the idea of the capital withdrawal plan described in chapter 7 may wish to use a number of funds including one that is heavily invested outside of Canada.

One of the best long term performers in Table #11 is Templeton Growth. Some mutual fund observers are nervous about this fund because it is run by John Templeton who is now well along in years. What will happen when Mr. Templeton no longer runs the fund is something that cannot be predicted. In addition, the 8.5% front-end load for Templeton Growth is not negotiable.

TABLE #11
AVERAGE ANNUAL COMPOUND RATE OF RETURN FOR NON-TAX SHELTERED MUTUAL FUNDS FOR THE PERIOD ENDING JUNE 30, 1986

AVERAGE ANNUAL COMPOUND RATE OF RETURN					
Company	Maximum sales charge	1 yr.	3 yr.	5 yr.	10 yr.
AGF Japan	9.0%	92.9%	39.9%	23.4%	24.3%
American Growth	9.0%	27.0	16.7	19.7	19.5
Bolton Tremblay Int'l.	9.0%	41.1	21.4	22.2	20.3
Dynamic American	Nil	22.3	18.2	18.4	
Investors International	8.5%	25.3	11.8	14.7	14.9
Investors Japanese	8.5%	87.9	32.1	21.2	22.5
Royal Trust "A"	Nil	31.8	12.3	14.2	13.7
Templeton Growth	8.5%	31.8	21.7	19.3	24.0
United Accumulative	9.0%	34.3	25.7	17.7	18.7

Notes: 1. Growth figures ignore sales charges
2. Templeton Growth sales charges not negotiable.

Source: *Financial Times,* July 21, 1986.

e. SUMMARY OF QUESTIONABLE SALES PRACTICES

The mutual funds, having become a much bigger player in the personal finance field, have also been engaged in some very questionable sales and marketing tactics. Some of these tactics have been those of the funds themselves and some have been those of independent mutual fund salespeople. Some of these practices have been mentioned in previous chapters. Here is a summary to help you keep in mind practices to watch for.

(a) The conflict of interest — some mutual funds salespeople have been holding themselves out as financial planners and/or advisors. You can sell mutual funds and you can sell advice but you can't sell both.

(b) Some quote performance figures that do not include sales commissions that must be paid.

(c) Some quote performance figures for the most favorable time period obtainable and change that time period when it suits the salespeoples' purposes.

(d) Some fail to include management fees in mutual fund sales literature.

(e) Some fail to advise consumers of the risks involved in the purchase of equity-based funds.

(f) Some fail to advise consumers that their investment is not protected by the Canada Deposit Insurance Corporation.

(g) Some sell funds for tax shelter purposes and fail to advise consumers that non-taxable capital gains and preferentially treated dividends will eventually be taxed as though they had been interest.

(h) Some try to persuade people to borrow large amounts of money to invest in mutual funds when they should be reducing their debts

(i) Some fail to advise consumers that sales charges are negotiable and imply that front-end loaded funds perform better than no-load funds.

(j) Some pressure senior citizens into buying mutual fund based registered retirement income funds when the senior citizens are not inclined to take any risk with their funds.

(k) Some distribute registered retirement income funds (RRIFs) literature that ignores the present value of money and that uses misleading annuity comparisons. (This problem will be somewhat reduced because of the new RRIF legislation proposed in the February 26, 1986 budget.)

(l) Some fund salespeople are peddling very questionable advice on how to get out of an RRSP "tax free." (See section i., chapter 7.)

If you still like equity funds, perhaps the following cautions will be of some help.

(a) Avoid funds that have been in existence for less than five years.

72

(b) Avoid funds that are very small (assets less than $1 000 000).

(c) Avoid very large funds — they tend to be poor performers.

(d) Avoid funds with loading charges or acquisition fees, except perhaps for non-tax sheltered funds. In that case, deal with a discount broker and don't pay more than 4%.

(e) Watch the high variability funds. Recent performance statistics may be misleading as the fund may have had a long way to come.

(f) Check the portfolio of the fund to get an idea of how many high risk stocks the fund plays with.

(g) Watch the *Financial Times* each month.

(h) Beware of advertisements that show performance data that ignore sales charges.

(i) Avoid both mutual fund salespeople and stockbrokers when buying mutual funds.

9

LIFE INSURANCE RRSPs

A fairly small portion of the dollar volume of registered retirement savings plans ends up with the life insurance industry. Many of the RRSP vehicles sold by this industry border on the disreputable and the consumer should be on guard against being taken in by one of the industry's representatives.

Life insurance companies use four basic vehicles or variations of them for registered retirement savings plans. These vehicles are cash value life insurance policies, deferred annuities, equity funds, and flexible contribution annuities.

a. WHY YOU SHOULD BE CAREFUL WITH LIFE INSURANCE EQUITY FUNDS

Generally speaking, the life insurance industry has managed the equity portion of its assets reasonably well. Although track records are hard to come by, the *Financial Post* survey of funds publishes a quarterly summary of the pooled equity funds managed by a number of life insurance companies.

A number of firms do very badly, but since the performance figures do not include front-end loading charges, it is impossible to compare them with the numerous Canadian mutual funds that are generally available to the public and compared monthly in the *Financial Times*.

The main reason why life insurance equity funds should be avoided is the front-end loading charges connected with them. Some of these loading charges are greater than the ones charged by some mutual funds described in chapter 7.

This is part of the reason why the price of many life insurance products is so high — they are sold by a sales force and that sales force has to be paid.

Unlike products sold by trust companies, banks, credit unions, and no-load mutual funds, life insurance products are "taken to the customer." This accounts for the high expenses incurred by the life insurance industry that are described later in the chapter.

Although it might be a simplistic explanation, in effect, an individual buys mutual funds "wholesale" from trust companies, banks, and no-load funds and "retail" from a life insurance company.

b. DEFERRED ANNUITIES

A deferred annuity is an arrangement whereby, in return for a certain sum or fixed annual sum for a certain number of years, an insurance company guarantees to pay the contributor a fixed income for life. The fixed income commences at an agreed time — usually around the age of 65. (You will remember that if the annuity is registered as a retirement savings plan, the income must commence no later than the end of the year in which you turn 71.)

The problem is that contributors receive only a nominal rate of return of their investments. An *average* of around 3-1/2% over a long period of time is about the rule. In the early years of the contributions, contributors will lose money if they change their minds and cash in their annuities.

By purchasing deferred annuities from life insurance companies, consumers may find themselves locked into those companies for the rest of their lives (or until they cash in their plans). Although they have a legal right to shop for life annuities, they most likely will not. In all likelihood, the life annuity will be automatically purchased from the same insurance company from which the deferred annuity was purchased. As will be shown later in the book, the price of annuities varies widely from company to company, and also from day to day.

c. THE DISADVANTAGES OF LIFE INSURANCE COMPANIES

1. Salespeople

Too many Canadians are using life insurance policies for their registered retirement savings plans. The disadvantages of doing this arise from the fact that many life insurance people do not understand their product, giving financial advice when they are hopelessly unqualified to do so. They are given short cram courses and then let loose on the unsuspecting public. (Another disadvantage arises from the unfavorable investment characteristics of life insurance policies. This will be discussed in chapter 11.)

2. Misleading language

You should also avoid life insurance companies because they arbitrarily re-define English words to suit their own interests, which further confuses consumers. An example of this arbitrary re-definition is the word "dividend." Normally, a dividend is a portion of the after-tax profits of a company that is passed on to the shareholders.

However, dividends from a life insurance policy are not dividends at all. They are merely partial returns of over-charged premiums. This fact is readily admitted by the authors of widely-used insurance textbooks. (Some of the authors were senior officers of large life insurance companies.)

3. Conflict of interest

Another reason why registered retirement savings plans should not be purchased from life insurance companies is that there is, in many cases, a conflict of interest between the company and the salespeople on the one hand, and the consuming public on the other. Policies that provide the most profit and leverage for the company are the most costly for the individual. They also result in higher commissions for the salespeople.

For example, most salespeople get a better reward for selling a cash value policy than they do for a term or pure insurance policy. In most cases, they also get a higher commission for selling a participating policy. A participating policy is a combination of reducing-term insurance and guaranteed cash surrender values, *plus* "dividends." A non-participating policy is the same thing, *minus* the "dividends." Annual premiums for participating policies are generally about 30% higher than for non-participating policies.

4. Inefficiency

A fourth reason why life insurance companies should be avoided is their scandalous inefficiency. The administration expenses of some life insurance companies can be many times greater than some well-known "no-load" mutual funds.

One of the striking characteristics of the evolution of the Canadian life insurance industry is the complete absence of a period of bankruptcy, merger, and consolidation of weak and inefficient firms that is normally characteristic of economic competition. As a result, these firms have continued to prosper and merrily sell their high-priced products.

There are, in my opinion, a number of reasons why such an evolution has not taken place; among them are the following:

(a) The messy public bankruptcy of an inefficient life insurance firm and its accompanying financial disaster for thousands of private citizens would not be tolerated by either industry or government for the simple reason it would bring unwanted public attention to the price of their products and the management of their firms.

(b) The "heads: the company wins and tails: the policyholders lose" nature of their product makes it virtually impossible for even the most sloppily-managed firm to lose money.

(c) The consuming public refuses to believe that there is a significant price variation for similar or identical products sold by different companies. Therefore, high-priced, inefficient companies continue to be patronized by naive consumers.

(d) It is inconvenient, expensive, and sometimes impossible for individual consumers to change companies even if they want to.

The result is that, without any real competition in the economic sense of the word, the life insurance industry is characterized by a number of small, inefficient firms. (A few of the large ones aren't very efficient either.) Their inefficiency is translated into high consumer prices for their products in general, and their participating cash value products in particular.

There are a number of special cases where smaller firms offer particular policies at particular ages at lower prices than the larger companies. However, a study of life insurance prices shows that, beyond a shadow of a doubt, the consuming public would clearly benefit from a rash of mergers of small companies with larger ones.

10

CASH VALUE LIFE INSURANCE POLICIES: BEWARE

a. RATE OF RETURN

First, as has been previously shown, the life insurance policy can average a long-term return of only about 3-1/2%. This figure excludes the cost of insurance protection, which is difficult to pinpoint. The best way to approximate this cost is to assume that it is about the same as the annual premium for a decreasing term-to-65 policy for the same face value as the cash value policy. Since cash value insurance is a combination of savings and decreasing term insurance, it follows that the actual cost of protection is equal to the insurance portion of the cash value policy, not the total face value. Decreasing term insurance is a type of insurance that decreases in coverage each year, while the premium remains constant.

To nail this reality down as tightly as possible, one has only to look at the return which the life insurance industry *nets* on its assets. Table #12 shows this net return for several companies.

b. CASHING IN OR TRANSFERRING

The second reason why cash value insurance policies are poor vehicles for registered retirement savings plans is that if consumers wish to cash in their plans in the early years or switch to another company, they will suffer a huge loss. Table #13 shows the cash surrender values and therefore the loss for $10 000 worth of three types of cash value insurance — whole life, life paid-up-at-65, and 20-payment life. It is assumed that all three policies were purchased from a well-known Canadian company, by a male aged 25.

TABLE #12
NET INTEREST EARNED FOR SOME
LIFE INSURANCE COMPANIES

Company	% Rate
Canada	11.95
Crown	10.65
Excelsior	11.78
Great West	11.31
Imperial	12.16
Industrial	11.47
Metropolitan	9.49
Mutual of Canada	12.25
New York Life	8.73
Prudential (America)	8.82
Sun	11.50

Source: Stone & Cox Insurance Tables, 1985.

TABLE #13
CASH SURRENDER VALUE FOR THREE YEARS
OF NON-PARTICIPATING CASH VALUE
INSURANCE FOR A MALE AGED 25
(Annual premium in brackets)

Years in force	Whole life ($115.80)	Life-paid-up at-65 ($153.60)	20-payment life ($208.10)
5	$ 160	$ 210	$ 460
10	650	840	1 430
20	2 060	2 530	4 060

c. PRICE VARIATION

The third reason why cash value insurance policies should not be used for registered retirement savings plans is that the price for identical products varies widely from one company to another. This usually comes as a surprise to everyone but the most sophisticated and informed individuals. The surprise usually comes after the consumer has paid into a life insurance policy for a number of years.

For purposes of illustration, assume that a consumer gets prices from a number of companies on their most inexpensive cash value policy — non-participating whole life.

Generally, cash value life insurance is broken down into three categories: whole life, limited payment life, and endowment. If you buy a whole life policy, you pay until you die, regardless of your age. (Whole life, the least expensive type of cash value insurance, is also known as ordinary life, straight life, and by a number of meaningless brand names that serve only to further confuse the policyholder.)

Limited payment life policies are more expensive than whole life. At a certain point they are "paid up." This means that the policy continues to build cash surrender values and pay dividends (if it is a participating policy) until the policyholder dies, regardless of age. After the policy is paid up, the policyholder does not have to pay any more premiums. The most popular type of limited payment life policy that is sold these days is the kind that is paid up at the age of 65. Some years ago, 20-payment life was often purchased, but it has lost consumer favor because of its high price.

The most expensive kind of cash value life insurance is endowment insurance. A life insurance policy "endows" when its cash value equals its face value. A widely-sold type of endowment policy is the 20-year endowment or "kiddie contract" sold to gullible parents of innocent children.

In any case, let us return to the assumption and examine the cost of a $10 000 non-participating policy for a male aged 25. Traditionally, the cost of life insurance was determined by taking a given time-period, multiplying the annual premiums by the number of years in the period, and then subtracting the cash surrender value and accumulated dividends (if any). This was known as the net cost method. Its disadvantage is quite obvious — it does not take into account the time value of money.

In recent years, the most widely used method of determining life insurance costs is the "interest-adjusted" method. It works like this:

(a) A given time period is selected, usually 10 years.

(b) The annual premium is multiplied by the factor by which $1 will grow over the 10-year period at a pre-determined interest rate. (The most commonly-used rate in Canada is 8%.)

(c) The cash surrender value at the end of the 10-year period is subtracted from the result obtained in step (b), and this result is divided by the factor used in step (a).

(d) If the policy is participating, the dividends are accumulated at the 8% rate, and they, too, are subtracted in step (c) along with the cash surrender value.

This price variation adds another dimension to the conflict of interest between the consumer and the industry, on the one hand, and the general public, on the other. Unlike the general insurance industry, the life insurance industry is pretty well saddled with the concept of single company representation. Even if salespeople know that they can get a customer a lower price from a competing company, they are unlikely to make the effort to obtain a special case agreement from the competitor and place the policy with the competitor. The fact that the high-priced companies continue to write new insurance proves that few single case agreements are obtained from lower-priced companies.

d. INABILITY TO KEEP UP PAYMENTS

A fourth reason why cash value insurance should be avoided is the bind that you will find yourself in if you are unable to keep up the payments on your policy because of extenuating financial circumstances caused by anything other than illness or disability. If this happens, your accumulated cash surrender value is used to buy "paid-up insurance." This paid-up insurance is usually a very small percentage of the face value of the policy. For example, in Table #13 the cash surrender value of the $10 000 non-participating whole life policy after five years is $160. This will buy only $600 worth of paid-up insurance.

On the other hand, if financial circumstances dictate that payments cannot be made to a mutual fund or trust company, no terrible problem results. The money stays there and continues to work for the consumer. It is not confiscated to buy a next-to-nothing, worthless, paid-up insurance policy.

e. THE ALLOWABLE LIMIT

A fifth reason why cash value life insurance policies should not be used for RRSP purposes is that the portion of the premium acceptable for registration (tax deductibility) by Revenue Canada may well have no relationship to the policyholder's RRSP limit. For 1986, for example, the limits are $3 500 and $7 500. It could be that because of increasing salary, the amount that could be contributed to an RRSP is well below the deductible portion of the premium. In 1987 and subsequent years this may not be so much of a problem for members of defined benefit pension plans because their annual RRSP limits will probably be fixed, in most cases at $2 000.

If an individual has a dramatic drop in salary, it is quite possible that little or no contributions could be made to an RRSP. But if the RRSP is a life insurance policy the premiums would have to be paid or the whole plan would collapse.

f. THE INSURANCE PORTION OF THE CONTRACT

If the insurance policy does not or has not endowed when the RRSP is turned into a form of life-time income, the insurance portion of the contract is terminated. The insurance portion is the difference between the face value (death benefit) and the cash surrender value. A life insurance policy endows when the cash value and face value are equal.

g. POOR RATE OF RETURN ON DIVIDENDS INVESTED

If the life insurance policy used for an RRSP is a participating policy, and chances are very good that it is, the dividends are automatically invested and re-invested in a form of savings account run by the life insurance company. The interest on these accounts is calculated and compounded annually and credited to the account only once a year. Sometimes the rate of interest is never disclosed on the annual statement. The rate is set, in most instances, early in the calendar year and not changed until the next annual revision, regardless of what happens to the general level of interest rates. Historically, the companies have paid rates far below those paid on similar investments.

h. GUARANTEED ANNUITY PRICES

As far as guaranteed annuity prices are concerned the salespeople's claims are true. However, because of the absurdly low interest rate earned by life insurance policies, the claim is irrelevant and also very foolish. To illustrate the point, suppose two individuals, aged 35, each bought a registered retirement savings plan, both contributed $1 000 per year to the plan, the contributions continued for 30 years, and each retired at 65. The first individual went the guaranteed annuity route and, for the sake of argument, averaged about 4% annual return on his $1 000. He will have accumulated $58 000 in his plan. The second individual went the mutual fund route and averaged about 8%, accumulating approximately $122 000. The difference was $64 000. Quite a sacrifice to make for a guaranteed annuity price!

i. MORE MYTHS DISPELLED: WAIVER OF PREMIUM

In defence of their product, the life insurance salespeople come up with some interesting arguments that involve the concepts of waiver of premium and guaranteed annuity prices.

Waiver of premium is, in effect, a long-term income protection rider attached to an insurance policy that guarantees the payment of premiums if the policyholder is unable to work because of illness or accident. One of the characteristics of long-term income protection is that, in general, the greater the restrictions on the definition of disability, the lower the premiums. Waiver of premium rates on life insurance are very low. From this, readers can draw their own conclusions. In addition, the waiver of premium concept is neatly contrived to make sure that disability income goes to the insurance company and not to the grocer, the milkman, or the dentist.

In any case, it is the responsibility of the individual to arrange his or her affairs so that he or she is able to receive some sort of salary even if disabled. This is achieved either by buying an income protection policy or by obtaining it through a place of employment that provides such a policy or some sort of cumulative sick-leave plan.

j. RECENT DEVELOPMENTS

There have been two recent developments in the life insurance industry that pertain to the cash value products the companies sell and to the registration of policies for RRSP purposes. Both the Canadian Life Insurance Association and the Life Underwriters Association of Canada have suggested strongly that salespeople not sell life insurance policies for RRSPs. This is probably because of a large number of consumer complaints about the practice. The complaints that the industry worries about most are those filed with the provincial superintendents of insurance. But they don't like television programs like *Marketplace* poking their noses into their rats' nests either.

The second development in the industry revolves around the interest adjusted method of calculating the cost of cash value life insurance policies. It is based on the assumptions that:

(a) Eight percent is a reasonable *after tax* rate of return on investment.

(b) Everyone has the same marginal tax rate.

(c) Everyone is either above or below $1 000 of investment income.

(d) Most people have extra cash laying around and have nothing better to do with it than to lend it to an insurance company in the form of the overcharge on a participating policy.

(e) Inflation does not exist. That is, dollars received from a life insurance policy in the form of dividends or cash surrender values have the same purchasing power as those originally paid to the companies in the form of premiums.

(f) Dividends (for participating policies) illustrated at the point of sale are paid or, if there is a variation, that variation is uniform for all companies and all age brackets.

As you can see, these assumptions are very shaky indeed. However, the industry persists in making them, casting further doubts about their credibility.

11
LIFE INSURANCE: FLEXIBLE CONTRIBUTION PLANS

One of the more recent developments in the RRSP field has been a relatively new product sold by life insurance companies. The product is usually called a single premium annuity and is being marketed by a number of companies.

There are several reasons why the life insurance industry is selling this product, among them the following:

(a) A large number of consumer complaints about their other RRSP products — life insurance policies and deferred annuities

(b) Increasing consumer sophistication

(c) An increasing amount of "shopping around" for RRSP products

(d) The aggressive entry of banks and credit unions into the RRSP field (Both of these institutions sell better products than anything any life insurance company has yet come up with.)

The life insurance companies' single premium annuities are very much like bank, trust company, and credit union plans in several respects. They do not require any more than one annual payment and pay an intermediate rate of return.

However, many of these plans pay rates of interest lower than those paid by deposit-taking institutions. In addition, these plans have other significant and unfavorable characteristics —two types of front-end loading charges and an impossible-to-calculate rate of return. These two features prevent all but the most sophisticated consumer from comparing the plans with those sold by banks, trust companies and credit unions. Unfortunately many of the life insurance salespeople and even some of the companies have engaged in a persistent campaign of misrepresentation in their sales pitches and even in what, in my opinion, is misleading newspaper advertising. But let's look first at the front-end load.

a. THE FRONT-END LOAD

Single premium annuities carry two types of front-end loading charges — a start-up fee and a salesperson's commission.

The start-up fee, which is usually $50 or $60, is a one time initial charge. But because some people feel more comfortable holding a number of RRSPs, this charge is a burden they must assume every time they buy a single premium RRSP.

The second component of the front-end load is the salesperson's commission — usually about 5% or 6% of the amount invested. This commission is flat, or uniform for all amounts invested — the initial and subsequent contributions. In my view, these charges are unnecessary for the consumer. You can get a better product commission-free at a trust company or credit union with no front-end load at all. In fairness to the life insurance industry, their salespeople have to be paid. If the companies began to bypass their sales forces they would be faced with considerable morale problems. Also, although I find the start-up fees and sales commissions objectionable, they are nowhere near the 9% charged by many mutual funds for lump sum investments. The commissions are also minimal when you compare them to the front-end load carried by a whole life insurance policy.

It also should be pointed out that fewer companies are charging this front-end load.

b. THE RATE OF RETURN

One of the most unfortunate aspects of the sale of single premium annuities is the way the companies and the salespeople deal with the rate of return. Nominally, it appears to be about the same as the rate paid by a trust company or credit union. Salespeople have been known to imply this is a true rate but when you look at it closely you will see that the initially attractive rate is paid *after* the sales and start-up charges are deducted. This has the effect of dramatically lowering the *true* rate of return.

For instance, one company advertised their rate as 9-1/8% for five years without mentioning in the ad sales commission or start-up charges. After allowing for the $50 start-up fee and 5% sales commission, the actual rate of return over the five years was almost 2% lower than the advertised rate.

The answer to this whole problem is quite clear. Since some companies will not reveal the true rate of return on their single premium annuities, they should be forced to do so by law.

c. COMPARISON TO TRUST COMPANIES

Another type of misrepresentation has been brought to my attention involving the comparison of single premium annuity RRSPs to trust company, credit union and bank products.

The salesperson says something like this, "Trust companies charge an annual management fee of 3/4% every year on the total amount you have invested. Our charges are deducted only once and if you add up the trust company management fees and compare them to our sales and start-up charges you will see that after five years our plans are more attractive." I know a chartered accountant who fell for that one.

In the first place, trust companies charge management fees on income, mortgage, and equity funds. They do not levy any management fees at all on their guaranteed plans that are identical to single premium annuities in every respect, except, in some cases, for the length of time that the interest rate is guaranteed. Credit unions usually levy no charges whatsoever. So to compare loading charges on a single premium annuity to management fees charged by trust companies is to compare apples and oranges and, as such, is inherently dishonest.

d. COMMISSION FREE ANNUITY PURCHASES

Another line used by life insurance salespeople when they are peddling RRSPs goes something like this; "Buy your RRSP from me and when it comes time to convert it to a life annuity, term certain annuity or registered retirement income fund, you can choose any one of those products and purchase it 'commission free' from my company."

At first it sounds pretty good, but let's look at the facts. Commissions on life annuities are very small. They vary from 2-1/2% to 4% of the purchase price of the annuity. Usually they are 3%. Commissions on term certain annuities sold by life insurance companies are about 1% of the amount involved. They can be obtained commission free from trust companies. At the time that I am writing this section, commissions on registered retirement income funds could not be determined. It would seem reasonable to assume that they could be obtained commission free from a number of sources because all issuers of RRSPs will be able to sell them so there would probably be no reason to buy them from a life insurance company.

The second reason why the "commission free" line is really a red herring involves the expected rate of return on investment. To illustrate, suppose we have two males age 45 who embark on an RRSP program. One buys a guaranteed RRSP from his credit union and one buys a single premium annuity from a life insurance company. Both invest $1 000 each year for 20 years and at age 65 they turn their lump sums into life annuities which they purchase from the same company that the second investor purchased his single premium annuities from. Suppose the true average yield from the credit union turned out to be 9% and 7% from the life insurance company — both reasonable assumptions.

After 20 years the total value of the credit union plan would be $55 764. The total value of the life insurance plan would be $43 865, a difference of $11 899.

But the whole thing doesn't end there. Another underlying assumption of the saving of the sales commission is that the company selling the single premium annuity will have the best life annuity rates 20 years from now. And that is patently ridiculous. Life annuity rates change daily and vary up to 60% from one company to another.

However, the February, 1986 budget dealt a blow to life annuities, making them a very unattractive RRSP termination option.

e. LIFE-INSURED RRSPs

Early in 1981, two major deposit taking institutions, the Bank of Montreal and Canada Trust, dropped a bombshell into the high-priced, high-powered promotional campaigns to sell RRSPs. With some limitations, these two organizations offered a "free" life insurance package to their RRSP customers. The protection required no submission of evidence of insurability, it took effect six months after the RRSP was purchased and remained in effect to age 60. If the planholder died while the coverage was in force, the amount of money in the RRSP (up to a maximum of $30 000) was matched by both Canada Trust and the Bank of Montreal.

The Bank of Montreal even had the audacity to take out full page national newspaper advertisements to invite consumers who had their RRSPs with other institutions to transfer their funds to the Bank of Montreal. (One of my colleagues tried and the bank personnel didn't know how to do it.)

As could be expected, the Canadian life insurance establishment had its predictable fit. They don't like any process that draws attention to the real cost of life insurance when the substantial marketing and selling expenses are eliminated. They contended that since nothing is free, a portion of the individual's contribution to the RRSP was used to purchase life insurance and was, therefore, not tax deductible. They couldn't seem to understand that the Bank of Montreal and Canada Trust were probably paying the cost (approximately $3 or $4 per $1 000 of coverage) out of the same pocket that was providing the funds for other promotional expenses such as radio and television advertising, pamphlets, signs, etc.

To illustrate, let's take the argument to its silliest extreme. Suppose the Bank of Montreal and Canada Trust gave away a pair of hockey tickets or a set of steak knives to everyone who purchased an RRSP. Should the fair market value of the tickets or the knives be subtracted from the amount of the contribution that is deductible for income tax purposes? What if these institutions provided free parking? Should a fair market value for the parking be deducted from the RRSP contribution? How silly!

However, Revenue Canada knuckled under to the pressure and said in October, 1981, that for the 1981 tax year and on, the banks may not issue an RRSP receipt for the fair market value of the insurance coverage portion of life-insured RRSP contributions.

It is now six years since this episode. Even though, in principle, life insuring RRSP contributions is a good idea, no one seems to have tried it again.

f. RECENT DEVELOPMENTS

In recent years, many life insurance companies have dropped the front-end load from their single deposit annuities. Public pressure and competition sometimes seems to work.

But instead of letting the matter drop, a large number of the life insurance companies extract their profits in other ways. One is by paying low interest rates. Another is the imposition of hefty withdrawal fees or penalties. Admittedly, consumers do not have to pay these withdrawal fees if they don't want to. But the investor may be placed in a position of having to forfeit a better deal elsewhere or pay the withdrawal fee. Not a very good choice.

To sum up the discussion of the use of single premium annuities for RRSP purposes, you can assume the following:

(a) The true rate of return almost invariably will be about 1-1/2 to 2% lower than the rate quoted for the net or final investment depending on the size of the investment if front-end loading charges are attached to the premiums.

(b) You may get sales pitches that are very misleading.

(c) The rate of return may be lower than you could get elsewhere.

(d) Since the profit and sales commissions on single deposit annuities are very low, anyone who buys one may be unwittingly walking into a pitch for another misleading life insurance product.

Not every life insurance company manages its single deposit annuities this way and it is unfortunate for those that do sell products that are every bit as good as their trust company and bank competitors. But they and they alone must clean up their act and until they do the best advice I can give you is, "DON'T BUY A REGISTERED RETIREMENT SAVINGS PLAN FROM A LIFE INSURANCE COMPANY."

12

TERMINATING YOUR RRSP

Before 1979, Canadians who had money in RRSPs were faced with a grim choice at retirement. Before the end of the year in which they turned 71 they either had to buy a life annuity or de-register their RRSP and pay tax on the de-registered funds. For most people, the life annuity was the only real choice. This seemingly unfair situation was generating a growing amount of very lucrative business for the Canadian life insurance industry. The RRSP terminations were supplemented by money purchase pension plans for retiring employees. These pensions were also in the form of life annuities. (In 1984, the last year for which data are available, the total amount of new life annuities purchased exceeded $3 billion.)

In 1979, the choices open to owners of RRSPs were expanded to include term certain to age 90 annuities and Registered Retirement Income Funds (RRIFs). The intention was to give consumers more choice and to allow financial institutions other than life insurance companies access to the growing pool of money in RRSPs. (Life insurance companies are the only organizations that can sell life annuities.)

Unfortunately, the term certain annuities to age 90 were rarely purchased because they paid out smaller monthly incomes than life annuities. RRIFs were also unappealing because they paid out very low monthly incomes in the early years. Most informed consumers still opted for the life annuity.

a. REGISTERED RETIREMENT INCOME FUNDS
In the February 26, 1986 federal budget, however, RRIFs were made much more attractive RRSP termination vehicles. The initial RRIF concept called for maximum monthly

payments that were very small. This was replaced by a new approach that called for minimum payouts. RRIFs instantly replaced life annuities as the best RRSP termination option for most people.

b. ADVANTAGES AND DISADVANTAGES OF RRIFs

1. Advantages

The most attractive feature of RRIFs is that they pay out more than annuities do. But there are also a number of other advantages:

(a) Consumers can choose their RRIFs from a range of investment vehicles almost as wide as that of investments for RRSPs.

(b) Consumers can manage their funds inside RRIFs to the same extent as they managed their RRSP funds.

(c) With the February 26, 1986 federal budget, consumers can choose as many RRIFs as they please. (Before that date only one RRIF per person was allowed.)

(d) In most cases, consumers can switch their RRSP to an RRIF with the same institution and use the same investment vehicle. All that is required is a little paperwork.

(e) As retirement or age 71 approaches, the decision to switch from an equity-based (common stock) RRSP to some type of guaranteed plan, because of apprehension of falling stock prices, does not have to be made.

(f) RRIFs allow money to be left to an heir while life annuities, in most cases, die with the annuitant(s).

2. Disadvantages

Even with their obvious advantages, RRIFs do have a downside. Among their disadvantages are the following:

(a) While most consumers can manage their funds and make investment decisions in their seventies, they may be unable to do so in their eighties.

(b) RRIFs sold by stockbrokers could present serious problems for unsophisticated consumers. Many stockbrokers' RRIFs consist of a pool of common stocks. It is in the financial interest of the brokers to do as much buying and selling as possible because they are paid by commission on both sales and purchases. But it may be in the consumer's interest either not to have a common stock-based RRIF, or if this route is chosen, to do very little trading of the shares.

(c) RRIFs sold by mutual funds also present problems because of some of the people who sell the funds. The front-end load (sales commissions) for the funds can be as high as 9% of the amount invested. There are perfectly good no-load funds that are sold directly to the consumer with no sales commission. In addition, mutual fund salespeople have been known to switch consumers' RRSP funds from one fund to another — for a big sales commission each time, of course. There is no reason to believe that this will not happen if the funds are transferred to an RRIF.

3. Summary
RRIFs are certainly a better deal than annuities. But they have to be managed with wisdom, expertise, and care. Unfortunately for the average consumer, there is little in in the way of impartial and independent advice on the issue. Most of the advice comes from the people who sell the product, which can be a serious problem and a conflict of interest.

c. WHICH RRIF SHOULD I CHOOSE?
Along with the pleasant changes in RRIFs come some problems. Chief among these problems is which one to choose and where and from whom to buy. Essentially the same range of choices confronts consumers as when they try to sort out the hundreds of RRSPs available.

The first step in choosing an RRIF is to decide what level of investment risk or combination of levels of risk is most acceptable or least unacceptable. At the high end of the risk scale is a pool or portfolio of common stocks. Unless the RRSP is in this form, this alternative probably should not be chosen. If it is, the consumer should probably consider downgrading this risk to a common stock-based (equity) mutual fund. If an equity-based RRIF is chosen, the consumer should avoid both stockbrokers and mutual fund salespeople and those who call themselves financial planners, consultants, or advisors. The top performing Canadian no-load mutual funds mentioned earlier in the book provide ample consumer choice for equity-based RRIFs.

If a mutual fund that invests in bonds or mortgages is chosen, the consumer will have to have a good handle on the inverse relationship between the values of these funds' units or shares and the general level of interest rates. As interest rates go up, the value of the funds' units goes down, and vice versa. Unless the consumer is prepared to identify and buy into these funds at the top of the interest rate cycle and get out at the bottom, then these funds are poor RRIF choices.

Many consumers will want all or part of their RRIF to be in the form of fixed income certificates. This means that choices must be made on the length of the interest rate guarantee. Many people like the idea of a 50/50 split: 50% in 1-year guarantees and 50% in 5-year guarantees.

Regardless of the choice, consumers who do a little work and some reading and who make an effort to stay on top of their situations will likely do much better with their RRIFs than those who do nothing.

d. ANNUITIES

There are two types of annuities that are used as termination vehicles for Registered Retirement Savings Plans — life annuities and term certain to age 90 annuities. Neither is very good and only one has any place at all in the scheme of retirement income.

1. Term certain to age 90 annuities

Term certain to age 90 annuities are sold mostly by trust companies, but are also issued by life insurance companies. They pay a fixed and guaranteed monthly income until the annuitant reaches age 90 and then the payments stop. The payment is almost the same as that from a joint and last survivor life annuity with a 10-year guaranteed payment period. (This type of annuity will be explained in the next section.) It is about 85% to 90% of the payment a male would expect to receive from a life annuity with a 10-year guaranteed payment period. (This annuity will also be explained in the following section of this chapter.)

The reason life annuities pay more than term certain to age 90 annuities is that the average annuitant is not expected to live to age 90 and therefore the life insurance company that issues the annuity can pay a larger income from it.

The major disadvantage of the term certain to age 90 annuity is the low monthly income. And if the annuitant lives beyond age 90 no more income is received. These two reasons, separately or together, should persuade consumers not to buy a term certain to age 90 annuity with their RRSP funds.

2. Life annuities

Prior to the February 26, 1986 federal budget, the life annuity was perhaps the best and most popular choice of people who had to terminate their RRSPs. The following are some of the most common variations of the life annuity.

(a) *Guaranteed-for-life annuities* are the annuities that pay the largest monthly incomes. The issuing life insurance companies agree to pay people holding this type of life annuity a monthly income as long as they live. If they die after receiving just one payment, their estates receive nothing. Guaranteed-for-life annuities are rarely sold.

(b) *Life annuities with cash refund guarantees* are much the same as guaranteed-for-life annuities. But if the annuitant dies shortly after purchasing the annuity, the estate or beneficiary receives the original amount paid for the annuity minus any payments received by the annuitant.

(c) *Life annuities with guaranteed payment periods* are more expensive than the previous two and pay out still lower monthly incomes. Common guaranteed periods are 5, 10 and 15 years. The period can also be guaranteed until the annuitant would have reached age 90. If a person purchases a life annuity with a 10-year guaranteed period and dies a year later, the issuing insurance company will continue to pay the monthly income to the annuitant's spouse for the remainder of the guaranteed period, in this case, 9 years. If the beneficiary is someone other than the annuitant's spouse, the payments are commuted.

The insurance industry would rather sell this type of annuity because it enables the companies to retain some of the deceased's money years after his or her death. This fits in well with the insurance game of taking people's money, keeping it for a long period of time, paying a low rate of interest on it and erecting as many barriers as possible to keep it from being returned to its rightful owners.

(d) *Joint and last survivor annuities* are the most expensive type of life annuity. They cover two lives, usually husband and wife. The issuing company guarantees to pay the monthly income until the death of the last of the two annuitants. A guaranteed period is usually built into these annuities, much to the advantage of the life insurance companies.

(e) *Impaired health annuities* are sometimes purchased by people in bad health. Because they have a statistically shorter lifespan, these people receive a somewhat higher payout.

Table #14 shows the monthly income paid from a selection of annuities in mid-1986.

TABLE #14
APPROXIMATE MONTHLY INCOME FROM
LIFE AND TERM CERTAIN ANNUITIES
PURCHASED WITH $50 000

Age at purchase	Single Life Annuity Guaranteed 10 Years Minimum		Joint Life Annuity Guaranteed 10 Years Minimum	Term Certain To Age 90
	Male	Female	Male and Female	Male and Female
60	$470	$445	$424	$424
61	475	449	427	427
62	480	454	431	429
63	485	459	435	433
64	491	464	439	440
65	499	469	444	444
66	505	475	449	449
67	511	481	455	454
68	518	488	461	459
69	525	496	467	466
70	532	503	474	473
71	542	509	481	482

3. Advantages of life annuities

Since the February 26, 1986 federal budget, there are only one or two advantages of life annuities worth mentioning. The income is fixed and guaranteed for as long as the annuitant(s) live. This makes budgeting and financial planning easier for some people. On-going financial investment and money management decisions are eliminated and the annuitants are not subjected to sales pressure from stockbrokers, mutual fund salespeople, etc.

4. Disadvantages of life annuities

There are major disadvantages to life annuities. They pay out very low incomes. For males at age 65, the income is about what they could get from a 5-year Guaranteed Investment Certificate. Why not buy an RRIF and preserve the capital? When life annuities are purchased, the capital is irrevocably surrendered to the life insurance industry. Life annuities discriminate against women. They receive about 7% less than men of the same age with the same amount of money to buy an annuity. With the eventual abolition (1990) of the right to roll retirement income back into an RRSP, the decision to buy a life annuity will have no relief from changes in interest rates. People will not be able to buy a life annuity and roll the monthly payments back into an RRSP to take advantage of changing interest rate levels. This is a problem if interest rates go up, but a blessing if they go down.

The only people life annuities may be appropriate for are those who are incapable of managing their affairs.

For those who still wish to buy a life annuity, it is important to use the services of an annuities broker or a person who acts as one. To check on annuity prices, it is a good idea to watch the Sunday edition of the *Toronto Star*. In his personal finance column, George Brett publishes annuity rates once a month. This is indeed a valuable consumer service.

13

DEFERRED PROFIT-SHARING PLANS

One of the lesser known and used tax shelters is the deferred profit-sharing plan (DPSP). It is used by small business corporations instead of a registered pension plan.

a. RECENT CHANGES

The May 23, 1985 budget proposed sweeping changes to DPSPs and their relationship to registered pension plans.

First, the most significant change was an increase to the tax deductible contribution limits for DPSPs from $3 500 to one-half of the maximum dollar limit for money purchase pension plans, which will be $7 750 in 1990. (Money purchase pension plans pay pensions based on a pool of money accumulated over the years as opposed to defined benefit plans where the pension is based on a combination of years of service and some sort of final average earnings.)

The budget also proposed dramatic changes in the vesting of DPSP contributions and how the funds can be invested. Vesting is the term used to describe funds contributed on an employee's behalf. The following are some more details of the proposed changes.

1. Plan combinations

Employers commonly provide retirement benefits to employees in money purchase plans and defined benefit form. The combination of a DPSP with a defined benefit registered pension plan is a typical example. The May budget proposed a new method of plan registration so the new limits on tax-assisted savings will be applied fairly. The plans will be acceptable for registration as long as the *total value of benefits* to an individual planholder in one year does not exceed the overall limits.

For example, an employer whose defined benefit registered pension plan has an effective benefit rate of 1.5% of earnings (3/4 of the 2% defined benefit limit) could also set up a DPSP with contributions of up to 4.5% earnings (1/4 of the 18% money purchase contribution limit). Various characteristics of the plan will be taken into account to determine the benefit rate. These include integration with the Canada or Quebec Pension Plan and the extent of automatic indexation and survivors' benefits. Contributions to an employer-sponsored money purchase plan will reduce the RRSP contribution room available under the $2 000 limit for defined benefit plan members.

2. Scope for profit-sharing arrangements

Under the budget proposals, profit-sharing arrangements will be more easily implemented due to an increase in the limit on deductible contributions to DPSPs from the current level of $3 500. By 1990, the DPSP limit will be 18% of earnings to a dollar maximum of $7 750 or half the overall limit of $15 500. DPSP contributions will reduce the contributions that can be made to other plans. Thus, for a DPSP member who also belongs to a money purchase registered pension plan and who also saves through an RRSP, the total contribution to the three plans cannot exceed 18% of earnings to the dollar maximum of $15 500.

DPSPs will be required to meet new conditions beginning in 1986. First, immediate vesting of new DPSP contributions will be required. Second, the proportion of new contributions on behalf of an employee which can be invested in shares of the employer will be limited to the greater of $3 500 or one-half the amount of the contribution. Third, an existing provision which allows the transfer of shares to a plan member at the deemed value of their cost to the plan will be modified. As a result, all benefits received from a DPSP will become taxable as ordinary income with the exception of the accumulated capital gain on employer shares transferred to the plan member. One-half of this gain will be taxable.

3. Contribution limits

Contributions to money purchase plans will be limited to 18% of earnings under the May budget. For employer-sponsored registered pension plans or DPSPs, the 18%

limit will apply to total remuneration in that employment. For RRSP contributions, the limit will be 18% of pensionable earnings less the total contributions to employer-sponsored plans. To provide transitional relief in 1986 and 1987, individuals who do not belong to defined benefit pension plans will be allowed to contribute to money purchase plans the greater of 20% of earnings, or $3 500 or $5 500 (whichever applies), or the new limit.

b. ELIGIBLE INVESTMENTS

Generally, the same investments that are eligible for RRSPs are also eligible for DPSPs. For this reason, the same selectivity process described elsewhere in this book for RRSPs should apply to DPSPs.

Since a number of different individuals are involved in these plans, they will, no doubt, have different investment needs and preferences. Conservative employees may prefer bond-based, guaranteed, or mortgage types of investments. Those who are more inclined to a little risk might like some type of equity-based investment. The closer that one gets to retirement, the more attractive safer investments become.

The fact that there may be a number of different investment preferences make it advantageous to look at the DPSPs sold by trust companies. Most of these organizations have several different investment alternatives for the funds of DPSPs. The most common are equities, bonds, mortgages, and guaranteed plans. Some companies have a combination of all four, and most allow credits in a DPSP to be switched from one alternative to another without penalty or charge. In addition, plan members may have simultaneous deposits in all four types of plans.

c. CHARGES AND FEES

Generally, it can be said that there is more paperwork associated with DPSPs than with RRSPs. As a result, administrative costs are generally higher. These fees are levied in one, some, or a combination of the following ways:

(a) Minimum initial charges on a flat basis
(b) Annual minimum charges on a flat basis
(c) Annual management fees expressed as a percentage of the total market value of the plan
(d) Front-end loading charges on initial and subsequent contributions, the load on initial money generally being higher than on subsequent contributions
(e) Annual flat fees for each member of the plan

d. COMMUNICATIONS

One aspect of a DPSP that should not be overlooked is the method by which the members are informed from time to time of the value of their share of the plan. Is the communication a meaningless annual computer printout? Or is it a quarterly easily-understood brochure that not only conveys the necessary information but also serves to help the employee identify with his or her plan and perhaps make him or her feel good about it.

e. CONTRIBUTION DATE

Unlike RRSPs, contributions to DPSPs can be made up to April 30 after the end of the year for which deductions are being claimed.

14
OTHER TAX SHELTERS

a. TREE FARMS
One of the least likely topics for a tax saving or tax postponement would have to be tree farms. Yet it is one of the most appropriate, effective, and interesting.

Revenue Canada has recently issued a lucid and fairly complete interpretation bulletin on the subject. The bulletin divides tree farms into three categories: woodlots, Christmas tree farms, and forest planting.

1. Woodlots
Many existing farms have a woodlot that generates a small portion of the total farm income. In this case, proceeds from the sale of logs, lumber, poles or Christmas trees are considered income from farming. Amounts received from permitting other persons to remove standing trees from the woodlot are considered to be on account of capital. Normally this has no tax consequence for the farmer but anyone in this situation should consult Revenue Canada bulletin IT-373R.

2. Christmas tree farms
Normally people who own Christmas tree farms are entitled to report their income by the cash method, which means that no income must be reported until it is earned.

The costs of purchasing and planting the trees are deductible as are expenses such as pruning, cultivating, fencing, property taxes, mortgage interest on the land, etc. Although Revenue Canada is silent on the matter in its bulletin, the following other deductions should apply in the situation.

(a) Wages to children

To the best of my knowledge, a tree farm is one of the few ways an unincorporated taxpayer, in a high tax bracket, can transfer some of his or her taxable income to a child where it is taxed at a much lower rate or perhaps not taxed at all.

The wages must be legitimately earned and the following guidelines should be observed.

(a) A diary showing dates and times of actual hours worked should be kept by the owner of the tree farm.

(b) The payments to children should be by cheque.

(c) The children must be old enough to do the actual work for which they are paid.

(d) The wages paid must be the same as those that would be paid to a stranger performing the same work.

Because of the amount of money that a child may earn (for 1986 it is $2 720) before the personal deduction for the taxpayer is impaired or eliminated, it is clearly advantageous for the wages to be paid to the children.

(b) Automobile expenses

It is not clear whether Revenue Canada will allow automobile expenses incurred by driving back and forth from the taxpayer's residence to the tree farm as allowable expenses. Before declaring such expenses it would be wise to check with your nearest Revenue Canada office.

Where tree sales are not reported by the sixth year after planting (or later, depending on local growth conditions) the taxpayer's operations may be viewed as a forest planting as described in the next section.

3. Forest planting

A taxpayer who is not otherwise engaged in a lumbering or logging business and who undertakes the re-forestation of an area of land with the objective of producing mature trees at a date that may be 40 or 50 years in the future, or even longer, can still be considered a tree farmer. Apart from the proceeds that may be obtained from the thinning of trees from time to time, no revenue can be expected until the trees mature. In the meantime, recurring costs for property taxes, looking after the trees, etc. must be paid. Whether these costs are deductible depends on whether the whole operation has a reasonable expectation of profit. If the facts indicate that the project was undertaken in a systematic way, is being conducted in a business-like manner in accordance with good forestry procedures, and holds forth the prospect of a profit when the trees mature, the loss created by these costs may be deducted as a business loss.

4. A reasonable expectation of profit

If losses from a tree farming operation or any other side-line business are to be deducted from other income, the farming operation must have a reasonable expectation of profit. If it turns out that this is not the case, Revenue Canada may disallow all of the losses that have been declared over the years. To avoid this situation, make sure to obtain enough land and plant enough trees so that income will exceed all losses declared.

5. Limits of losses

The losses resulting from the operation of a tree farm that can be deducted from "other income" are not unlimited. In any given year, the first $2 500 are totally deductible and one half of the next $5 000 are also deductible. Losses in excess of these limits are not deductible and must be absorbed by the taxpayer.

6. The farming aspect

Now let's have a brief look at the silviculture of the operation. Arrangements for planting trees will differ from province to province and each province publishes information on the subject. For example, in Ontario these guidelines are printed in the booklets *Private Land Forestry Service* and *Planning for Tree Planting* and are available from the Ontario Ministry of Natural Resources. Check with the provincial department responsible for land use where you live for further information.

b. FILMS

One of the catchy tax shelters that has come to public attention in recent years is Canadian films. Individuals have apparently been using these vehicles for tax postponement. At the time this is being written, the tax treatment of some aspects of film investment is still pretty much up in the air. So, before you get into a film investment, make sure you get a written ruling on the tax aspects of the investment before you take the plunge.

In addition, it is wise to look at a film investment from the same point of view as a MURB (see chapter 16 on MURBs). Ask the question, "Is the film itself a good investment or do I need the tax break to make it worthwhile?" If you need the tax break, look very carefully at it.

In the short period of time that they have been eligible for tax shelter, movies have become quite a big business, although only one Canadian film in twenty makes a profit.

What has been happening in the movie business is similar to what has been happening in the oil and gas exploration game. Film-makers are selling shares or units to the public through stockbrokers. When I was writing this section I obtained information on two movies. Generally, the prospectus for each was very much the same. The following are some of the bits and pieces of information in each document.

(a) Price per unit
(b) Number of units being sold
(c) Description of the films including —
    (i)   Plot synopses
    (ii)   Principal artists
    (iii)   Producers
    (iv)   Directors
    (v)   Authors
(d) Budget summary
(e) Use of proceeds
(f) Interim financing
(g) Nature of the investment
(h) Making the film

(i) Commercial exploitation

(j) Theoretical range of box office receipts

(k) Income tax implications

(l) Speculative nature of the investment

(m) Unit holders' agreement

Generally unit holders are entitled to receive 100% of the producers' gross up to the purchase of the units and 50% of the producers' gross thereafter.

There are about six sources of revenue for films:

(a) Theatres

(b) Network television

(c) Television syndication

(d) Pay television

(e) Inflight exhibition

(f) Schools and other institutions

It would seem reasonable that 60% of theatre box office receipts might come from the U.S., 7% from Canadian showings and 33% from foreign showings. This points out the need for some arrangement for the film to be shown in the U.S.

There are several points that you should consider before going into a film investment.

(a) Make sure that the film qualifies for the 100% capital cost allowance (50% the first year and 50% the second year).

(b) Make sure the prospectus is at least under consideration (or preferably approved) by a reputable securities commission.

(c) Make sure that some arrangements for distribution have been signed before you invest.

(d) Deal with a broker you respect and trust.

(e) If you don't know anything about movies check with some people who do.

(f) Realize that, at this time, there is a non-existent market for movie units if you want to sell out.

The concept of investing in films revolves around two points: capital cost allowance and leveraging.

1. Capital cost allowance

There are three classes into which films fall for purposes of capital allowance — 100%, 60% and 30%.

Obviously, the 100% class is most attractive from an investment point of view. There is no difference between films and videotapes for capital cost allowance purposes. The 100% capital cost allowance is awarded to a "certified Canadian production" that meets certain criteria. Since only half the capital cost allowances may be declared in the year the asset is purchased, the deduction for movies, videotapes, etc., will be 50% of the purchase price in the year of acquisition and 50% the next year.

2. Certified Canadian productions

A certified feature film is defined as a film certified by the Secretary of State to be not less than 75 minutes in running time. The photography or art work specifically required for production of the film must have been started after November 18, 1974 and been completed before May 26, 1976. After May 26, 1976, both film and videotape features can qualify for certification as can short Canadian films or videotapes under 75 minutes in length. One of two further requirements for certification must also be met. The production of the film or videotape must either result from a co-production agreement between Canada and another country or the film or videotape must meet *all* of the following criteria.

(a) It must be produced by a Canadian.

(b) A portion of the creative personnel, to be determined by the Secretary of State and fixed by regulation, must be Canadian.

(c) 75% of the total remuneration paid in connection with the production, except what is paid to persons referred to in (b) and for final processing and preparation, must be paid to Canadians.

(d) 75% of all costs incurred in the final production must result from services performed in Canada.

(e) The copyright must be beneficially owned by Canadian individuals or federally or provincially incorporated companies.

For "tax savings" purposes, it is not worth talking about films that depreciate at less than 100%. However, if you are interested, you can refer to bulletin IT-283 issued January 19, 1976.

3. Other tax points

A capital cost allowance can only be claimed for a given year if the principal photography for the film is completed during that year or during a period of up to 60 days after the end of that year.

Also, keep in mind that losses generated by capital cost allowance may not necessarily be write-offs. They may only be an interest free loan from the government as is the case for most MURBs. If the film is sold for more than the "depreciated" or "book" value, which in the case of the film is zero, then there will be a capital cost recapture. That is, the tax benefit of the loss will have to be repaid.

If the film is sold for more than its original price, the difference will be a capital gain. But since capital gains will soon virtually escape taxation, this issue should be ignored.

c. YOUR OWN HOME

Perhaps the greatest tax shelter of all is your own home. In most cases there are no capital gains taxes on the home when you sell it. As you live in it, you also get some enjoyment — a bonus economists call psychic income.

In addition, a mortgage on the home can be reduced from time to time without penalty. By reducing the mortgage you are really investing in an asset that will not attract tax when it is eventually sold. In this respect, it is a much better tax shelter than a registered retirement savings plan.

For individuals who have investment income of less than $1 000, the difference in interest between an individual's mortgage rate for one year and a one-year savings certificate is not much. But when you get above the $1 000 investment, reducing the mortgage on a personal residence becomes much more attractive than investing the money. For example, if you are in a 40% marginal tax bracket, you have to gross 20% to net 12%.

While it is not necessarily a tax shelter, you should try to get a mortgage that allows you to make payments when you want to instead of once a month. For example, if you have a 25-year $50 000 mortgage at 13%, paying one-half the monthly payment every two weeks will reduce the total interest paid over the life of the mortgage by more than $45 000, and the house will be paid off in 17 years rather than 25 years.

1. Cottages and retirement homes

Prior to the May 23, 1985 budget, capital gains tax was an issue most people thought about before purchasing either cottages or retirement homes or both. In most cases an unknown amount of capital gains tax would have had to be paid when these assets were eventually sold. For the most part, this is no longer the case because the budget allows for a $500 000 lifetime exemption on capital gains. Cottages and retirement homes are now a much better investment than they were before the budget.

2. Renting your home

Again, prior to the May 23, 1985 budget, if you rented all or part of your home you were liable to a capital gains tax when the home was eventually sold. The capital gain was on the portion of the house that was rented. If a person rented two rooms of a six-room house to students for two years that person would have to declare a capital gain of two-sixths of the amount that the house appreciated in value during the period that the rooms were rented. Fortunately, for most people this headache has been eliminated.

d. MUTUAL FUNDS AND SAVING FOR YOUR CHILD'S EDUCATION

Most parents and grandparents, at one time or another, think about a systematic savings program for a child's or grandchild's education. Essentially, there are four popular approaches to this strategy: putting the money into a savings account, GIC or Savings Bond; buying a life insurance policy for the child; buying a Registered Educational Savings Plan, such as the ones sold by the Canadian Scholarship Trust or University Scholarships of Canada; and buying a mutual fund.

1. Savings accounts

Putting the money in a savings account has two major disadvantages. First, the interest rate is usually quite low, particularly until sufficient amounts accumulate to buy a Canada Savings Bond or Guaranteed Investment Certificate. Second, because interest attracts tax at the full marginal rate, a substantial income tax liability could accrue sometime for the contributor.

2. Life insurance policies

Buying a life insurance policy for the child is probably the worst possible plan. Typical policies sold for this purpose are of the 20-year endowment variety. They should be avoided for the following reasons:

(a) The rate of return on the investment portion of the contract is very low, not disclosed, and impossible to calculate accurately.

(b) Price comparison between similar policies sold by different companies is virtually impossible.

(c) If the child should die, the savings component of the policy (the cash surrender value) reverts to the insurance company.

(d) When the child needs the money for post-secondary education, a life insurance salesperson may attempt to convince the child to use the funds accumulated in the policy to buy another life insurance policy and thus the funds may not be used for the purpose for which they were intended — to finance higher education.

3. Registered Educational Savings Plans

Registered Education Savings Plans (RESPs) such as those sold by the Canadian Scholarship Trust and University Scholarships of Canada are becoming quite popular. If the plan is commenced before the child's first birthday, it is sold in units as low as $9 per month. For a small additional fee, the payments can be life insured so if the sponsor dies, the payments are made by the life insurance company. When the child turns 18, all of the contributions, less a small administrative charge, are returned. If the child successfully completes the first year of a qualifying post secondary program, he or she is eligible for a maximum of three further scholarships. These scholarships are equal, prorated portions of all of the interest earned by all of the funds on deposit during a recent one-year time period. Lately they have been exceeding $1 500 per scholarship. This represents about an 11% rate of return on the sponsor's investment.

While these RESPs are far better than nothing, they have some disadvantages:

(a) If the child does not attend a post-secondary program, all of the interest on all of the contributions is lost.

(b) The scholarships are taxable in the child's hands. Even if the child has no taxable income, receipt of the scholarship could reduce or eliminate the child as a dependant for a supporting parent. If this happens, the RESP has turned tax-free income into taxable income.

(c) These RESPs discriminate against students who attend community colleges. The programs offered by these institutions are typically two or three years in duration and, as a result, students are restricted to a maximum of two scholarships as opposed to three for the student who takes a four-year program at university. This disadvantage also applies to a student who takes a three-year pass degree at an Ontario university.

4. Mutual funds

Perhaps the best way for parents to save for a child's education is through a common stock mutual fund. Many of the funds will take investments in the form of monthly automatic bank withdrawals of small amounts — sometimes as low as $15. The following are a number of advantages of this approach:

(a) Almost all mutual fund appreciation is in the form of capital gain which, for most Canadians, is tax free.

(b) Over many years the Toronto Stock Exchange Index has outperformed treasury bills by about 4%.

(c) Good Canadian mutual funds have averaged about 19% in the long term.

e. HOUSEBOATS

Before the May 23, 1985 budget, houseboats were fast becoming Canada's hottest tax shelter. People who purchased these boats could write off huge losses against other income. These losses were generated by a huge capital cost allowance (depreciation). The allowable depreciation on fixed assets was 33-1/3% on a straight line basis. Almost all other depreciation on fixed assets is lower than 33-1/3% and is calculated by the much less attractive declining balance method. (For an explanation of the declining balance method see chapter 15.)

Suppose a person bought a $60 000 houseboat on May 1, 1985, for example. The allowable depreciation for 1985 would have been $6 667. For both 1986 and 1987, it would have been $20 000 and for 1988, $15 333.

The houseboat tax shelter scheme began to unravel on May 23, 1985. Boats bought after that date cannot have losses resulting from depreciation written off against other income. The situation worsened when news reports began to surface that perhaps Revenue Canada would not allow the 33-1/3% straight line depreciation on boats purchased *before* the budget came down. At the time of writing this issue had not been resolved.

There are two additional problems associated with the houseboat tax shelter. First, they are not tax savings plans; they are tax postponements. All of the depreciation claimed must be taken back into income when the boat is sold — if a buyer can be found. Second, tax advice from people who sell houseboats must be viewed with some skepticism.

f. NURSING HOMES, YACHTS, RECREATIONAL VEHICLES, AND HOTELS

Again, before May 23, 1985, such diverse items as yachts, recreational vehicles, nursing homes and hotels were being financed by selling limited partnerships in the ventures. The attraction, like houseboats, was that losses resulting from depreciation (capital cost allowance) could be written off against other income. The depreciation was not as generous as that allowed for houseboats but the schemes were being made to look attractive.

The May 23 budget effectively wiped out this shelter for individuals who are not personally active in the day-to-day operation of the business. Capital cost allowances that may be claimed by a partnership in such a business will also be restricted unless those partners who are personally active in the business of the partnership are entitled to share in at least two-thirds of the income and loss of the partnership for the year.

These new regulations will take effect beginning with the 1986 taxation year and will apply to property acquired after May 22, 1985 unless the property is acquired before 1986 pursuant to a written agreement entered into before May 23, 1985. A special transitional rule will apply to buildings acquired before 1987 pursuant to a written agreement entered into before May 23, 1985 provided construction proceeds without undue delay.

g. FORWARD AVERAGING

The forward averaging provisions of the Income Tax Act allow qualifying taxpayers to elect to spread certain eligible income received in the current year over future years when they might be in a lower tax bracket.

The eligible income is excluded in calculating taxable income but tax is nevertheless paid on it AT THE HIGHEST MARGINAL RATE — usually 50%. The eligible income and the tax paid on it is carried forward to following years.

A taxpayer may then elect to report all or any part of this income in any subsequent year and claim an appropriate share of the tax previously paid as a credit against tax otherwise payable in that year.

Forward averaging is a very complicated process. Only individuals who expect a dramatic drop in taxable income should even consider forward averaging. The drop in marginal tax brackets would have to be substantial to offset the earning power of the amount of money that must be sent to Revenue Canada to be used as a tax credit in future years. If the money has to be borrowed the drop in marginal tax rate will have to be even greater.

For more information, contact your nearest Revenue Canada office on forward averaging.

h. SUMMARY OF TAX SHELTER DANGERS
Because there has been so much advertising and public discussion of tax shelters, it is important to summarize the dangers and disadvantages of these shelters. People who advertise and sell them only present the advantages. Most of the problems with these tax shelters concern the deduction of losses resulting from depreciation against other income. The following is a list of potential problems.

(a) Revenue Canada may not allow the losses at all.

(b) In the vast majority of cases the shelters are not tax savings plans at all. They are tax postponements.

(c) If the shelter or asset is sold for more than its purchase price a capital cost re-capture occurs. This means that the difference between the selling price and the depreciated or "book" value must be taken into income in the year the asset is sold.

118

(d) The only tax relief for the income referred to in (c) is forward averaging. This relief requires a cash payment to Revenue Canada of 50% of the amount to be averaged and the taxpayer may be in the position of having to borrow this money.

(e) Many of the things being sold as tax shelters are overpriced because of their tax shelter gimmick.

(f) Many individuals and organizations selling tax shelters are holding themselves out as tax advisors as well. They have a clear and usually undisclosed conflict of interest.

(g) There is usually no after market for most tax shelters. When was the last time you saw an ad for a used MURB?

(h) If you die your survivors may find that they will have to include all of the depreciation that you have claimed in your final tax return without even the relief of forward averaging.

Before people buy a tax shelter they should ask themselves the question, "Would I buy this item if there were no tax advantages connected with it?" If the answer is no, then it should not be purchased.

15

SIDELINE BUSINESSES

Thousands of Canadians engage in some form of business activity in addition to their regular jobs. Thousands of housewives supplement their family's income with part-time jobs. Such activities are almost as numerous as the people engaged in them. They sell Amway and Avon, Tupperware and Fashion Magic. They do freelance writing and photography. They weave, do macrame and pot. And it's safe to say that most of them do not take advantage of all the items they can write off for tax purposes. By taking advantage of the deduction of all of the legitimate business expenditures to which they are entitled, they will either substantially reduce their taxable income or create a loss that can be legitimately used to deduct taxable income from other sources.

There is one thing that must be kept in mind when you are thinking of starting a small business. The tax department insists that the venture be undertaken with a reasonable expectation of profit. Selling the proverbial lawn mowers to Eskimos doesn't count.

In addition to the usual business expenses — supplies, office stationery, repairs on equipment, etc. — there are three areas of substantial tax savings that most people overlook: use of an office or workshop in the home, use of the family automobile for business purposes, and capital cost allowance on equipment.

Here is how you go about claiming your fair share of these items.

a. USE OF THE OFFICE OR WORKSHOP IN THE HOME

Provided you have a room in your home set aside for your business activity, you are entitled to deduct fair costs for that room. For example, suppose we use the case of the Avon lady. She and her husband live in a three-bedroom, five-room bungalow and she uses one of the bedrooms exclusively for business purposes. In it she keeps her inventory and records. She has shelving, a filing cabinet, desk, desk chair, office chair, and a typewriter. She bought them new for a total of $600.

Now let's look at what the tax department will allow her to claim as the cost for her office. First of all she has to keep records and receipts for all of the operating expenses of the house and submit a statement that looks something like this:

HOUSEHOLD EXPENDITURES 198-

Mortgage interest	$2 500
Property taxes (before homeowner's grant deducted)	800
Repairs	200
Insurance	150
Telephone (excluding long distance)	150
Heating oil	500
Water	100
Electricity	150
Number of rooms in house — 5	$4 550

Rooms used for business purposes — 1
Total business cost of office in home 1/5 of $4 550 = $910

b. USE OF THE FAMILY CAR FOR BUSINESS

Like the office in her home, the Avon lady also uses her automobile for business purposes — delivering orders, making sales calls, going to the post office, and so on. She should keep a diary and make specific notes of each business trip she takes and how many kilometres that she drives on business.

Then she should make up a statement that would look something like this:

STATEMENT OF AUTOMOBILE EXPENSES 198-

Gasoline and oil	$1 000
Repairs	200
Tires	100
Licence	40
Insurance	200
Car washes	20
Parking	20
Carrying charges	400
Capital cost allowance	1 500
Total operating cost for year	$3 480

Total number of kilometres driven = 15 000
Total cost per kilometre = 23.2¢
Total kilometres driven on Avon busines = 1 000
Total business cost of car = $232

c. CAPITAL COST ALLOWANCE

You will note that a strange and rather large item called capital cost allowance was included in the statement of automobile expenses. Capital cost allowance is the taxation term for depreciation. Depreciation is the rate at which an asset "wears out." The tax department allows a certain amount of this annual wearing out to be deducted as a business expense each year.

There are many different rates at which assets can be depreciated but for purposes of the Avon lady only two are relevant — 20% and 30%. She can depreciate her $600 worth of office furniture at the rate of 20% per year on the "declining" balance. That is, for the first year she can claim 20% of the $600 or $120 as a business expense. This will leave a "book value" of $480. Next year she can claim 20% of the $480 or $96, and so on down the line. (This applies to most types of machinery — looms, potters' wheels, cameras, etc. See chapter 16 for more information on depreciation classes.)

122

For automobiles the rate is 30% and it was assumed that the original cost of the Avon lady's car was $5 000 ($1 500 = 30% of $5 000).

There are some other points that must be kept in mind when calculating capital cost allowance.

(a) You must complete schedule 9 and return it with your tax form.

(b) Only one-half of one years' depreciation may be taken for the year in which the asset is purchased.

The other interesting item in the statement of automobiles that requires some amplification is carrying charges. This refers to interest paid on money borrowed to buy the car. In addition to being a deductible expense there is another important point raised by this item. That is, if you are going to purchase two items — one that cannot be used to earn income and one that can — borrow the money for the one that can be used to earn income and use your cash for the one that can't. The effect is negligible in the case of the Avon lady whose use of the automobile amounted to one-fifteenth of the total annual distance driven. But where the ratio of business to personal use is higher, deducting the interest as an expense dramatically lowers the true rate of interest paid.

In any case there is one cardinal rule that should never be violated: KEEP RECEIPTS.

16

MURBS

One of the most important and overlooked tax postponements can be found in the real estate field. They are multiple unit residential buildings and are more commonly known by their acronym — MURBs.

In order to explain how MURBs work you have to go back to the good/bad old days prior to 1972 when you could write off against other income, losses that were created in whole or in part from depreciation on rental buildings. What people were doing was buying rental properties late in the year and writing off huge losses against one month's income. Depreciation, for tax purposes, is calculated in a strange way. Unless you're actually in the apartment rental business full time, it doesn't matter what time in the year you acquire an asset for you to write off a whole year's depreciation. This loophole was closed in 1972 when losses caused by including depreciation in the financial statement were not allowed to be written off against other income.

The government changed its mind again in 1974. Depreciation on some rental buildings could again be used to create a loss to be written off against other income. The reasoning behind the change was to encourage medium and high income individuals to put their money into apartment buildings to help relieve the housing shortage.

a. THE CLASS 32 ASSET

The Income Tax Act provides that owners of multiple unit residential buildings that qualify as a Class 32 asset may claim a 5% capital cost allowance (depreciation) on those assets that may create or increase losses arising from these assets for income tax purposes. These losses may be used to offset taxable income from other sources.

124

To qualify as a MURB, Revenue Canada requires evidence in writing that the project was underway before November 18, 1981 AND that the footings were in place no later than May 31, 1982.

In addition, you must attest that —

(a) not less than 80% of the floor space will be used in providing self-contained domestic establishments and related parking, recreational, service and storage areas, and

(b) not more than 20% of the floor space is used for any purpose other than the purposes referred to in (a).

In November, 1982, Revenue Canada announced that the "undue delay" clock would not start ticking until January 1, 1983. As a result, projects that qualify for MURB status in all other respects would continue to do so if construction proceeds without undue delay.

In mid-1986 there were still some MURBs being advertised and sold.

b. WHAT IS DEPRECIATION?

Almost everything we buy that has any lasting value will some day be worthless and will have to be replaced. The tax department allows us to "write off" as a business expense each year a certain portion of many types of assets. The rate at which we are allowed to write off an asset is supposed to be approximately equal to the rate at which the asset "wears out."

There are many different rates at which we are allowed to write off assets. These rates are called classes and there are dozens of them. For purposes of this discussion let's use four — 5%, 10%, 20% and 30%. The following are examples that the tax department allows:

Class 3 (5%) buildings made of brick, cement or stone

Class 6 (10%) buildings made of frame, log, stucco on frame

Class 8 (20%) machinery and equipment not included in any other class

Class 10 (30%) automobiles

Generally the rate at which assets "wear out" is close to what the tax department allows. However, buildings seem to be an exception. Instead of declining in value they have tended to increase. This has important implications for tax savings as opposed to tax postponement. Since the depreciation allowance is tax deductible it would appear to be a "tax saving." But it is really only a paper saving. Since buildings increase in value, the tax "saved" by writing off depreciation will have to be repaid when the building is eventually sold. Therefore losses that result from declared depreciation are really tax postponements.

c. WHAT ARE THE RISKS?

Investing in real estate is no exercise for amateurs. It is a highly competitive field. Such things as changes in economic conditions (particularly in one-industry towns), the imposition of rent controls, changes in the property values in the neighborhood, provision of other attractive housing alternatives in the same community, changes in interest rates (particularly if the mortgage interest on the property is not fixed for the duration of the mortgage), changes in property tax rates, operating expenses, vacancy rates and "acts of God."

Apartment buildings are not like a mortgage-based trust company RRSP. You can't put them in your pocket and take them across the country. Neither can you change them into bonds, equities or fixed income securities with the stroke of a pen.

d. WHAT ARE THE BENEFITS?

The first and most apparent benefit is tax postponement by using the losses caused by depreciation. These are not tax savings but are nevertheless attractive for two reasons:

   (a) The tax postponed should be considered an interest-free loan from the government until it is repaid.

(b) The tax postponed will be repaid in inflated dollars that will, in all probability, constitute a smaller portion of the income of the taxpayer at the time the MURB is sold. But, the tax may have to be paid in a very high tax bracket.

e. INCOME
The other source of income from the MURB is what is left from rental income after expenses have been paid.

f. THE FRONT-END COSTS
Another attractive feature of MURBs is that a number of soft or front-end costs can be deducted and so help to create tax losses in the first year of ownership. Here are some examples of these costs:

(a) Interest and property taxes incurred by the developer
(b) Fees paid for the guarantee of a second mortgage if any
(c) Landscaping
(d) Certain legal fees
(e) CMHC mortgage insurance and application fees

MURBs are much more attractive tax postponement alternatives than RRSPs for a number of reasons.

(a) There is no limit to the amount that can be invested.
(b) The possibility of growth for the amount of risk taken is greater than for most RRSPs.
(c) If the plan is collapsed, i.e., the building sold, there are more flexible options to deal with the payback of tax benefits.
(d) There is no age limit imposed on the realization of benefits without oppressive taxation as there are with RRSPs (age 60).
(e) MURBs provide for partial distribution of earnings while RRSPs do not.

g. WHAT KIND OF RETURN CAN YOU GET FROM A MURB?

This question is almost impossible to answer. It depends on so many variables:

(a) What will the vacancy rate be?

(b) How much will rentals increase?

(c) What is the marginal tax bracket of the investor?

(d) How many front-end costs are "written off" in the first year?

(e) Is the tax postponed and saved invested at a profit? If so, at what rate?

(f) When will the MURB be sold?

The only answer seems to be that a good MURB is a very good investment.

h. DISADVANTAGES OF MURBs

The number of MURBs that are available is diminishing because of the time limit on the beginning of construction of the building. But this has not diminished the enthusiasm of the people who sell them.

When is the last time that you saw an ad for a used MURB? Buying a MURB is much easier than selling one and you may be in for a hard time if you want to bail out.

The tax burden on disposal may be quite a surprise. You will have to include all of the depreciation that you have declared in the year that you sell the MURB. Your only tax relief will be forward averaging and to obtain this relief you have to pay 50% of the amount to be averaged up front. (This 50% can be used as a tax credit in future years.)

There have been disturbing reports that people who sell MURBs have been overestimating revenues and under-estimating interest rates and other costs. Other horror stories imply that the MURBs are overpriced and the sellers have been getting away with this overpricing because of the alleged tax benefits of the deal.

And finally, there is some indication that MURB sales-people are holding themselves out as financial planning consultants and tax advisors. You can sell advice or you can sell MURBs but you can't sell BOTH!

17

ALTERNATIVES TO TAX SHELTERS

One of the most discouraging and frustrating aspects of the tax advising occupation is the strange and often irrational behavior of the public at large. There are thousands of people who will get down on their hands and knees and crawl miles over broken glass for a small tax saving or tax postponement. Few of these same people will bat an eye when they are handed financial information that can save them tens of thousands of dollars on everyday personal financial transactions. Some of this information is more valuable than available tax shelters.

a. MORTGAGE PLANNING

The most dramatic example of this problem is the mortgage payment plan offered by most credit unions and caisses populaires, some trust companies, and some banks. The plan, which should be attracting hundreds of homeowners and prospective home buyers, allows weekly and bi-weekly payments as well as monthly payments. In addition, depending on the institution, extra payments on the outstanding balance of the loan are allowed at certain times. The savings in interest are phenomenal.

The Canadian Imperial Bank of Commerce, for example, put out a brochure on the plan when interest rates on mortgages were about 13%. The brochure uses, as an example, a $50 000 25-year mortgage with monthly payments of $551.20. By paying $137.80 per week instead of $551.20 per month, the total interest paid over the life of the mortgage was reduced by $45 585.00. By paying $275.60 every two weeks, the reduction was almost as great — $45 089.00. In both cases the 25-year debt was totally repaid in slightly less than 17 years.

There are two reasons for this dramatic reduction in interest payable. First, the weekly payments of $137.80 for 52 weeks means that the equivalent of one additional monthly payment of $551.20 is made each year. Second, payments are made more quickly than the traditional one payment per month mortgage arrangement.

Essentially, in the monthly payment arrangement, funds lie around in the homeowner's chequing account for a number of days each month before the mortgage payment is deducted. These funds neither earn nor save interest for the homeowner. They are, in effect, borrowed interest-free by the lending institution. The weekly and bi-weekly payment plans transfer this interest from the lending institution to the homeowner. Over the life of the mortgage in this example, over $45 000 of this interest accrues to the homeowner at the expense of the lending institution and that is why very few of them offer this privilege.

Also, many lending institutions allow the homeowner to make extra payments on the outstanding balance of the mortgage at certain designated dates and times, usually on the anniversary date. This arrangement can also have a significant effect on the amount of interest paid. For example, extra annual payments of $1 000 can reduce the term of the mortgage described above from 16.7 years to 12 years, if payments of $137.80 are made weekly. The additional payments of $1 000 per year result in a further interest saving of almost $23 000. But the biggest savings by far are realized from the weekly payment plan and, given a choice, consumers should do business with firms that allow BOTH weekly or bi-weekly payments AND generous extra payments on principal.

Many banks and trust companies are now allowing weekly and bi-weekly payments. Most credit unions and caisses populaires have allowed these open mortgages for years. Homeowners with mortgages with these institutions have been allowed to make virtually unlimited payments on outstanding principal. But there are some drawbacks to dealing with the credit unions and caisses populaires. Many are reluctant to lend more than 75% of the appraised value of the home. This eliminates the segment of the market that does not have a down payment of 25% of the value of the home.

b. LIFE INSURANCE

Life insurance is one of the least understood of all financial planning products. Millions of consumer dollars are wasted on one of the most essential tools of financial planning. There are a few ways you can either save substantial amounts of money on this product or obtain much more coverage for the same cash layout.

1. Shop the market

A number of firms across Canada are now computerizing the rates for about 60 companies. This information, which is continuously updated, is franchised out to life insurance brokers across the country. The brokers then present customers with a computerized printout of the prices for the customer's age, sex, smoking rating, and the amount of insurance they need or want. Not only should consumers obtain a printout from one of these data banks, they should avoid, at all costs, any life insurance salesperson who is tied to one company.

2. University alumni plans

Almost every university in Canada provides a group life insurance plan for its members. In many cases, it is not necessary to have graduated from the university, only to have attended. Of course, to obtain coverage, one must join the organization. Most plans also provide access to the coverage to the members' spouses and dependants. Some also provide additional accidental death coverage. Most of the plans are underwritten by North American Life. Table #15 summarizes the rates and features of these plans.

There are a number of drawbacks to the North American Life Alumni Association plans. One is that they are expensive. Lower cost coverage might be obtained from one of the brokers described in the previous section. But

TABLE #15
ANNUAL PREMIUMS PER $1 000 OF COVERAGE FOR
NORTH AMERICAN LIFE ALUMNI ASSOCIATION
GROUP LIFE PLANS

	SMOKER		NON-SMOKER	
Age bracket	Male	Female	Male	Female
Under 30	$1.50	$1.20	$1.10	$ .80
30 — 34	1.80	1.40	1.20	1.00
35 — 39	2.40	1.80	1.50	1.10
40 — 44	3.90	2.90	2.10	1.70
45 — 49	5.90	4.40	3.20	2.50
50 — 54	8.70	6.40	4.80	3.40
55 — 60	13.00	9.00	8.00	6.00

Notes:
1. Some universities have maximum coverages less than $240 000 with the lowest being $200 000. For coverages lower than $240 000 the annual premium is adjusted proportionately.
2. Maximum coverage is $240 000.
3. Coverage is sold in units of $30 000.
4. Members' spouses may obtain up to $240 000 of coverage.
5. The coverage is convertible.

that would involve dealing with a life insurance salesperson and one of the very good reasons for going to an alumni plan is to avoid that.

The second drawback is that the $240 000 limit seems unreasonably low. Queen's University, which has the best alumni association plan in Canada, has very low prices, no maximum coverage and accidental death coverage included in the premium. In my opinion, it is about time that North American Life brought all of their professional and association plans into line with the Queen's University plan.

3. Association group life insurance
A large number of Canadian professional associations provide their members with group life plans. These plans range from very good to very poor. Some of the plans have rates much higher than those available on the open market.

Some have ludicrously low maximum coverages. Some provide no coverage for spouses. Some provide no reduction for women and/or for non-smokers. Still others charge twice as much as they should and then give the overcharge back in the form of a dividend after they have invested the overcharge for a year or more.

Table #16 shows the rates for the plan offered by North American Life to the following 12 groups:

Geological Association of Canada
Canadian Institute of Surveying
Ontario Association of Municipal Clerks and Treasurers
Canadian Association of Physicists
Canadian Association of Social Workers
Canadian Pulp and Paper Association
Canadian Psychological Association
Canadian Physiotherapy Association
Canadian Opthological Society
Canadian Institute of Planners
Canadian Paediatric Society
Canadian Purchasing Management Association

4. Cashing in existing coverage

To examine this situation, let's look at two imaginary men, Bill Jones and Tom Smith. Both purchased $10 000 participating whole life policies from London Life when they were 25 years old. Smith bought his in 1965 and Jones bought his in 1975. Both are still in good health and neither has smoked cigarettes for at least one year. The following is a summary of their respective policy situations.

	Smith	Jones
Annual Premiums	$ 151.30	$ 148.70
Cash Surrender Value	2 450.00	966.00
Accumulated Dividends	1 342.40	365.10
Total Policy Value	$3 792.40	$1 331.10

The numbers given for Smith and Jones are lower than a real situation because it is impossible to determine how

TABLE #16
ANNUAL PREMIUMS PER $1 000 OF COVERAGE FOR TWELVE PROFESSIONAL ASSOCIATIONS

Age bracket	NON-SMOKER		SMOKER	
	Male	Female	Male	Female
Under 30	$1.25	$1.00	$1.75	$1.25
30 — 34	1.38	1.13	1.88	1.50
35 — 39	1.50	1.25	2.38	1.88
40 — 44	2.13	1.75	3.75	2.88
45 — 49	3.25	2.50	5.88	4.38
50 — 54	4.75	3.50	8.75	6.25
55 — 59	7.50	5.63	13.13	8.75
60 — 65	8.75	6.25	17.50	10.00

Notes:
1. Coverage reduces after age 65
2. Conversion privilege available
3. Waiver of premium — included
4. Spousal coverage — maximum $200 000
5. Minimum coverage — $20 000
6. Maximum coverage — $200 000

much interest would have been earned by the dividends that were left on deposit.

Let's look at Smith first. If he cashes in his policy he will have to take about $800 into investment income. This will be a tax issue if he has more than $200 of investment income in the year the policy is cashed in. But he should go ahead anyway because he could invest the money at 10% and with the interest alone he could buy about $50 000 of term-to-100 coverage and pocket his annual premium of $151.30 for the rest of his life.

In the case of Jones, he would have no tax complications as a result of cashing in his policy. With the interest on his $1 300 and change he could buy about $36 000 of the term-to-100 plan. If Smith and Jones were smokers, they could buy $33 000 and $18 000 respectively.

If Smith and Jones wanted to add their annual premiums to the interest on their withdrawn funds, their coverage would be even more dramatically increased. For Smith, the coverage would now be about $73 000 if he were a non-smoker and about $48 000 if he smoked. For Jones, the figures would be $81 000 and $47 000 respectively.

Smith and Jones could either contact a life insurance broker or contact a representative of Transamerica Occidental, a company that pioneered the term-to-100 concept. Both Smith and Jones should be advised never to cancel an existing life insurance policy until the new one is delivered.

c. THE PROBLEMS OF LIFE INSURANCE AS A TAX SHELTER

For many years life insurance salespeople have been trying to persuade consumers that the purchase of cash value life insurance is a way to avoid tax on investment income. Cash value life insurance is a combination of life insurance protection and a savings program. As the savings program builds up it attracts no income tax. If the policy is participating, it carries an increased annual premium. (Usually the increase is about 30%.) Out of this overcharge the companies pay "dividends." These dividends are not taxed because they are not corporate profits, but partial refunds of the overcharged premiums.

There are a number of important points that must be made with respect to cash value life insurance policies and the income tax implications for the policyholders.

1. Stealing the savings

It is true that the buildup of savings in the form of cash surrender values attracts no tax either at death or while the policy remains in force. (This is not necessarily the case if the policy is terminated after a number of years or if a policy loan is taken out.) However, when the policyholder dies, the life insurance company simply takes the savings portion (the cash surrender value). Does it really make sense to postpone tax on an investment if you lose the investment when you die?

2. The poor rate of return

The rate of return on the savings portion of the contract is so low relative to the rate for similar investments sold by banks and trust companies that any tax saving is academic. It doesn't make any sense to sacrifice 5% on the rate of return for a small tax saving.

3. Possible tax consequences

If a life insurance policy is cashed in and the proceeds are greater than the amount paid to the company over the life of the policy, the difference is taxable as investment income. This is another reason why consumers should do their saving and investing with an organization other than a life insurance company.

4. What happens to dividends left on deposit?

The "dividends" from participating cash value life insurance policies are often left on deposit with life insurance companies in a type of savings account. Many companies have enormous sums of these "dividends" on deposit and they constitute a huge source of cheap money for the industry. At the end of 1982, the last year for which figures were available, the total amount of policyholders' funds on deposit in Canada exceeded $2.9 BILLION.

For years, the companies have been paying a rate of interest substantially below prevailing market rates on these deposits.

In addition to these very poor rates of return, there are a number of other problems associated with leaving policyholders' funds on deposit with life insurance companies. Since disclosure is voluntary, a number of large and well known firms simply don't publish their rates. Some companies don't even disclose the rates to their policyholders. The annual statement shows the amount of interest paid but not the rate.

However, another and perhaps more serious problem with policyholders' funds on deposit concerns income tax.

There is apparently no requirement to issue T-5 slips for less than $100 of interest earned in any given year. It can therefore accumulate and could eventually force the policy-holder over the $1 000 limit of tax-free investment income, thus attracting tax at the full marginal rate in some future year.

5. The rate of compounding
Despite the move to daily compound interest rates by most deposit taking institutions, the Canadian life insurance industry has lagged far behind. In almost every case, interest on dividends on deposit is declared, paid and compounded only once a year. This can make a substantial difference in long term yields. For example 12% compounded annually becomes 12.74% when compounded daily.

6. Conclusion
The bottom line is NEVER buy a tax shelter from a life insurance company and NEVER mix savings and/or investments with life insurance.

d. UNIVERSAL LIFE
Recently, there have been a number of articles and stories in the American financial press about a relatively new life insurance product. Called Universal Life, the product is in effect an unbundling of the traditional whole life policy. In universal life, the savings and insurance or protection elements are kept in separate accounts. The old whole life policies, which continue to be sold in large numbers in both Canada and the U.S., have savings and protection mixed together. Separating them out is like trying to get the gin out of a martini.

For decades, the life insurance industry scoffed at the idea of buying term insurance and investing the difference between the term premium and what whole life would have cost. Now they have seen the light and are selling just such a combination.

However, there are some very important caution lights that consumers should pay attention to before buying a universal life policy.

It is unlikely that the universal life policy will have an insurance component that is as reasonably priced as what could be obtained on the open term market. It is also unlikely that the savings element will be as attractive as what could be arranged outside the insurance contract, particularly after front-end loading and sales costs have been taken into consideration.

In the U.S., universal life is sold as an income tax deferral scheme. No tax is payable on the investment income earned until the policy is cashed in. That makes sense — for Americans. Unlike Canadians, they cannot receive their first $1 000 of investment income tax-free. They also have a capital gains tax so that investment in mutual funds is, other things being equal, not nearly as attractive to Americans as it is to Canadians. In addition, their allowable contributions to Individual Retirement Accounts (IRAs) are much lower than what Canadians are allowed to put into their RRSPs. If the new American Tax Code is approved as agreed upon in late August, IRAs will be even more restrictive.

It still makes more sense for Canadians to be adequately covered by proper term insurance, make maximum contributions to their RRSPs, pay down their debts and keep most of their interest bearing investments inside their RRSP. Investments outside RRSPs, except those required to earn that first $1 000 of investment income should be in some form of relatively safe equity-based mutual fund or a selection of safe common stocks.

While most articles in the American financial press are useful and accurate, there are some important cases such as universal life where American advice is considerably less than helpful to Canadians.

SELF-COUNSEL SERIES

CANADIAN
ORDER FORM
SELF-COUNSEL SERIES

10/86

NATIONAL TITLES:

_____ Abbreviations & Acronyms	5.95
_____ Aids to Independence	11.95
_____ Asking Questions	7.95
_____ Assertiveness for Managers	8.95
_____ Basic Accounting	5.95
_____ Be a Better Manager	8.95
_____ Best Ways	5.50
_____ Better Book for Getting Hired	9.95
_____ Between the Sexes	8.95
_____ Business Guide to Effective Speaking	6.95
_____ Business Guide to Telephone Systems	7.95
_____ Business Writing Workbook	9.95
_____ Buying (and Selling) a Small Business	6.95
_____ Civil Rights	8.95
_____ Collection Techniques for the Small Business	4.95
_____ Complete Guide to Being Your Own Home Contractor	19.95
_____ Conquering Compulsive Eating	5.95
_____ Credit, Debt, and Bankruptcy	7.95
_____ Criminal Procedure in Canada	14.95
_____ Design Your Own Logo	9.95
_____ Drinking and Driving	4.50
_____ Editing Your Newsletter	14.95
_____ Entrepreneur's Self-Assessment Guide	9.95
_____ Family Ties That Bind	7.95
_____ Federal Incorporation and Business Guide	14.95
_____ Financial Control for the Small Business	6.95
_____ Financial Freedom on $5 a Day	7.95
_____ For Sale By Owner	4.95
_____ Forming/Managing a Non-Profit Organization in Canada	12.95
_____ Franchising in Canada	6.50
_____ Fundraising	5.50
_____ Getting Elected	8.95
_____ Getting Sales	14.95
_____ Getting Started	11.95
_____ How to Advertise	7.95
_____ How You Too Can Make a Million . . . In the Mail Order Business	8.95
_____ Immigrating to Canada	14.95
_____ Immigrating to the U.S.A.	14.95
_____ Importing	
_____ Insuring Business Risks	3.50
_____ Keyboarding for Kids	7.95
_____ Landlording in Canada	12.95
_____ Learn to Type Fast	9.95
_____ Managing Your Office Records and Files	14.95
_____ Managing Stress	7.95
_____ Media Law Handbook	6.50
_____ Medical Law Handbook	6.95
_____ Mike Grenby's Money Book	5.50
_____ Mike Grenby's Tax Tips	6.95
_____ Mortgage and Foreclosure Handbook	6.95
_____ Musician's Handbook	7.95
_____ Parents' Guide to Day Care	5.95
_____ Photography & The Law	7.95
_____ Practical Guide to Financial Management	6.95
_____ Ready-to-Use Business Forms	9.95
_____ Resort Condos	4.50
_____ Retirement Guide for Canadians	9.95
_____ Small Business Guide to Employee Selection	6.95
_____ Start and Run a Profitable Beauty Salon	14.95
_____ Start and Run a Profitable Consulting Business	12.95
_____ Start and Run a Profitable Craft Business	10.95
_____ Start and Run a Profitable Home Typing Business	9.95
_____ Start and Run a Profitable Restaurant	10.95
_____ Start and Run a Profitable Retail Business	11.95
_____ Start and Run a Profitable Video Store	10.95
_____ Starting a Successful Business in Canada	12.95
_____ Taking Care	7.95
_____ Tax Law Handbook	12.95
_____ Tax Shelters	
_____ Trusts and Trust Companies	3.95
_____ Upper Left-Hand Corner	10.95
_____ Using the Access to Information Act	5.95
_____ Word Processing	8.95
_____ Working Couples	5.50
_____ Write Right!	(Cloth) 5.95 / (Paper) 5.50

PROVINCIAL TITLES:

Please indicate which provincial edition is required.

Divorce Guide
☐B.C. 9.95 ☐Alberta 9.95 ☐Ontario ☐Manitoba ☐Saskatchewan

Employee/Employer Rights
☐B.C. 6.95 ☐Alberta 6.95 ☐Ontario 6.95

Fight That Ticket
☐B.C. 5.95

Incorporation Guide
☐B.C. 14.95 ☐Alberta 14.95 ☐Ontario 14.95 ☐Man./Sask. 12.95

Landlord/Tenant Rights
☐B.C. 7.95 ☐Alberta 6.95 ☐Ontario 7.95

Marriage & Family Law
☐B.C. 7.95 ☐Alberta ☐Ontario

Probate Guide
☐B.C. 12.95 ☐Alberta 9.95 ☐Ontario 11.95

Real Estate Guide
☐B.C. 7.95 ☐Alberta 7.95 ☐Ontario 7.95

Small Claims Court Guide
☐B.C. 6.95 ☐Alberta 7.50 ☐Ontario 7.50

Wills
☐B.C. 6.50 ☐Alberta 5.95 ☐Ontario 5.95

Wills/Probate Procedure
☐Man./Sask. 5.95

PACKAGED FORMS:

Divorce
☐B.C. 9.95 ☐Alberta 10.95 ☐Ontario ☐Man. ☐Sask.

Incorporation
☐B.C. 12.95 ☐Alberta 12.95 ☐Ontario 14.95

☐Man. 14.95 ☐Sask. 14.95 ☐Federal 7.95

☐Minute Books 16.50

Probate
☐B.C. Administration 14.95 ☐B.C. Probate 14.95 ☐Alberta 14.95 ☐Ontario 15.50

☐Rental Form Kit (B.C., Alberta, Ontario, Sask.)   5.95

☐Have You Made Your Will?   5.95

☐If You Love Me Put It In Writing   Contract Kit   14.95

☐If You Leave Me Put It In Writing   B.C. Separation Agreement Kit   14.95

NOTE: *All prices subject to change without notice.*

Books are available in book and department stores, or use the order form below.

Please enclose cheque or money order (plus sales tax where applicable) or give us your MasterCard or Visa Number (please include validation and expiry date.)

(PLEASE PRINT)

Name _____

Address _____

City _____ Province _____ Postal Code _____

☐Visa / ☐MasterCard Number _____

Validation Date _____ Expiry Date _____

If order is under $20.00, add $1.00 for postage and handling.

Please send orders to:

INTERNATIONAL SELF-COUNSEL PRESS LTD.   ☐Check here for free catalogue.
306 West 25th Street
North Vancouver, British Columbia
V7N 2G1